AAT

GOWER COLLEGE SWANSEA

KU-071-752

TYCOCH

SWANSEA SA2 9EB

Qualifications and Credit Framework (QCF)

LEVEL 3 DIPLOMA IN ACCOUNTING

COMBINED TEXT AND QUESTION BANK

Professional Ethics in
Accounting and
Finance

2012 Edition

Second edition June 2012

ISBN 9781 4453 9723 8

British Library Cataloguing-in-Publication Data
A catalogue record for this book is available from the British
Library

Published by

BPP Learning Media Ltd
BPP House
Aldine Place
London
W12 8AA

www.bpp.com/learningmedia

Printed in the United Kingdom

Your learning materials, published by BPP Learning Media Ltd,
are printed on paper sourced from sustainable, managed forests.

All our rights reserved. No part of this publication may be
reproduced, stored in a retrieval system or transmitted, in any
form or by any means, electronic, mechanical, photocopying,
recording or otherwise, without the prior written permission of
BPP Learning Media Ltd.

©
BPP Learning Media Ltd
2012

CONTENTS

Introduction

Text

Question bank

Index

A NOTE ABOUT COPYRIGHT

Dear Customer

What does the little © mean and why does it matter?

Your market-leading BPP books, course materials and e-learning materials do not write and update themselves. People write them: on their own behalf or as employees of an organisation that invests in this activity. Copyright law protects their livelihoods. It does so by creating rights over the use of the content.

Breach of copyright is a form of theft – as well as being a criminal offence in some jurisdictions, it is potentially a serious breach of professional ethics.

With current technology, things might seem a bit hazy but, basically, without the express permission of BPP Learning Media:

- Photocopying our materials is a breach of copyright

- Scanning, ripcasting or conversion of our digital materials into different file formats, uploading them to Facebook or emailing them to your friends is a breach of copyright

You can, of course, sell your books, in the form in which you have bought them – once you have finished with them. (Is this fair to your fellow students? We update for a reason.)

And what about outside the UK? BPP Learning Media strives to make our materials available at prices students can afford by local printing arrangements, pricing policies and partnerships which are clearly listed on our website. A tiny minority ignore this and indulge in criminal activity by illegally photocopying our material or supporting organisations that do. If they act illegally and unethically in one area, can you really trust them?

BPP LEARNING MEDIA

BPP LEARNING MEDIA'S AAT MATERIALS

Since July 2010 the AAT's assessments have fallen within the **Qualifications and Credit Framework** and most papers are now assessed by way of an on demand **computer based assessment**. BPP Learning Media has invested heavily to ensure our ground breaking materials are as relevant as possible for this method of assessment. In particular, our **suite of online resources** ensures that you are prepared for online testing by allowing you to practise numerous online tasks that are similar to the tasks you will encounter in the AAT's assessments.

The first part of this **Combined Text and Question Bank** covers all the knowledge and understanding needed by you, with numerous illustrations of 'how it works', practical examples and tasks for you to use to consolidate your learning. The majority of tasks within the texts have been written in an interactive style that reflects the style of the online tasks the AAT will set.

At the back of this **Combined Text and Question Bank** there are additional learning questions corresponding back to the Text, plus the AAT's practice assessments and two BPP practice assessments. Full answers to all questions and assessments, prepared by BPP Learning Media Ltd, are included. Our question bank section of this Combined Text and Question Bank is also available in an online environment. This enables you to practise online tasks that are similar to the tasks you will encounter in the AAT's assessments.

BPP's range of resources available for Professional Ethics in Accounting and Finance comprises:

- **Passcards**, which are handy pocket-sized revision tools designed to fit in a handbag or briefcase to enable you to revise anywhere at anytime. All major points are covered in the Passcards which have been designed to assist you in consolidating knowledge.

- **Lecturers' resources**, providing a further bank of tasks, answers and full practice assessments for classroom use, available separately only to lecturers whose colleges adopt BPP Learning Media material. The practice assessments within the lecturers' resources are available in both paper format and online in e format.

This Combined Text for Professional Ethics in Accounting and Finance has been written specifically to ensure comprehensive yet concise coverage of the AAT's new learning outcomes and assessment criteria. It is fully up to date as at June 2012 and reflects both the AAT's unit guide and the practice assessments provided by the AAT.

Each chapter contains:

- Clear, step by step explanation of the topic

- Logical progression and linking from one chapter to the next

- Numerous illustrations of 'how it works'

- Interactive tasks within the text of the chapter itself, with answers at the back of the book. In general, these tasks have been written in the interactive form that students can expect to see in their real assessments

- Test your learning questions of varying complexity, again with answers supplied at the back of the book. In general these test questions have been written in the interactive form that students can expect to see in their real assessments

The Question Bank at the back contains these key features:

- tasks corresponding to each chapter of the Text. Some tasks are designed for learning purposes, others are of assessment standard

- the AAT's practice assessments and answers for and further BPP practice assessments

The emphasis in all tasks and test questions is on the practical application of the skills acquired.

If you have any comments about this book, please e-mail paulsutcliffe@bpp.com or write to Paul Sutcliffe, Senior Publishing Manager, BPP Learning Media Ltd, BPP House, Aldine Place, London W12 8AA.

A NOTE ON TERMINOLOGY

On 1 January 2012, the AAT moved from UK GAAP to IFRS terminology. Although you may be used to UK terminology, you need to now know the equivalent international terminology for your assessments.

The following information is taken from an article on the AAT's website and describes how the terminology changes impact on students studying for each level of the AAT QCF qualification.

What is the impact of IFRS terms on AAT assessments?

The list shown in the table that follows gives the 'translation' between UK GAAP and IFRS.

UK GAAP	IFRS
Final accounts	Financial statements
Trading and profit and loss account	**Income statement or Statement of comprehensive income**
Turnover or Sales	Revenue or Sales Revenue
Sundry income	Other operating income
Interest payable	Finance costs
Sundry expenses	Other operating costs
Operating profit	Profit from operations
Net profit/loss	Profit/Loss for the year/period
Balance sheet	**Statement of financial position**
Fixed assets	Non-current assets
Net book value	Carrying amount
Tangible assets	Property, plant and equipment
Reducing balance depreciation	Diminishing balance depreciation
Depreciation/Depreciation expense(s)	Depreciation charge(s)
Stocks	Inventories
Trade debtors or Debtors	Trade receivables
Prepayments	Other receivables
Debtors and prepayments	Trade and other receivables
Cash at bank and in hand	Cash and cash equivalents
Trade creditors or Creditors	Trade payables

UK GAAP	IFRS
Accruals	Other payables
Creditors and accruals	Trade and other payables
Long-term liabilities	Non-current liabilities
Capital and reserves	Equity (limited companies)
Profit and loss balance	Retained earnings
Minority interest	Non-controlling interest
Cash flow statement	**Statement of cash flows**

This is certainly not a comprehensive list, which would run to several pages, but it does cover the main terms that you will come across in your studies and assessments. However, you won't need to know all of these in the early stages of your studies – some of the terms will not be used until you reach Level 4. For each level of the AAT qualification, the points to bear in mind are as follows:

Level 2 Certificate in Accounting

The IFRS terms do not impact greatly at this level. Make sure you are familiar with 'receivables' (also referred to as 'trade receivables'), 'payables' (also referred to as 'trade payables'), and 'inventories'. The terms sales ledger and purchases ledger – together with their control accounts – will continue to be used. Sometimes the control accounts might be called 'trade receivables control account' and 'trade payables control account'. The other term to be aware of is 'non-current asset' – this may be used in some assessments.

Level 3 Diploma in Accounting

At this level you need to be familiar with the term 'financial statements'. The financial statements comprise an 'income statement' (profit and loss account), and a 'statement of financial position' (balance sheet). In the income statement the term 'revenue' or 'sales revenue' takes the place of 'sales', and 'profit for the year' replaces 'net profit'. Other terms may be used in the statement of financial position – eg 'non-current assets' and 'carrying amount'. However, specialist limited company terms are not required at this level.

Level 4 Diploma in Accounting

At Level 4 a wider range of IFRS terms is needed, and in the case of Financial statements (FNST), are already in use – particularly those relating to limited companies. Note especially that an income statement becomes a 'statement of comprehensive income'.

Note: The information above was taken from an AAT article from the 'assessment news' area of the AAT website (www.aat.org.uk).

BPP LEARNING MEDIA

ASSESSMENT STRATEGY

The Professional Ethics in Accounting and Finance (PEAF) assessment is normally a 1.5 hour computer based assessment.

The assessment is split into two sections, consisting of eight tasks in Section 1 and ten in Section 2, which will include a broad range of topics across the assessment criteria for this unit.

Competency

Learners will be required to demonstrate competence in both sections of the assessment. For the purpose of assessment the competency level for AAT assessment is set at 70 per cent. The level descriptor in the table below describes the ability and skills students at this level must successfully demonstrate to achieve competence.

QCF Level descriptor	Summary
	Achievement at level 3 reflects the ability to identify and use relevant understanding, methods and skills to complete tasks and address problems that, while well defined, have a measure of complexity. It includes taking responsibility for initiating and completing tasks and procedures as well as exercising autonomy and judgement within limited parameters. It also reflects awareness of different perspectives or approaches within an area of study or work.
	Knowledge and understanding
	■ Use factual, procedural and theoretical understanding to complete tasks and address problems that, while well defined, may be complex and non-routine
	■ Interpret and evaluate relevant information and ideas
	■ Be aware of the nature of the area of study or work
	■ Have awareness of different perspectives or approaches within the area of study or work
	Application and action
	■ Address problems that, while well defined, may be complex and non routine
	■ Identify, select and use appropriate skills, methods and procedures
	■ Use appropriate investigation to inform actions
	■ Review how effective methods and actions have been

Autonomy and accountability

- Take responsibility for initiating and completing tasks and procedures, including, where relevant, responsibility for supervising or guiding others

- Exercise autonomy and judgement within limited parameters

BPP
LEARNING MEDIA

AAT UNIT GUIDE

Professional Ethics in Accounting and Finance (PEAF)

Introduction

This unit guide relates to the Level 3 Unit on Professional Ethics in Accounting and Finance. It should be read in conjunction with the NOS standards and QCF standards for this unit. The aim of this guide is to provide further detail and additional advice for tutors delivering the Professional Ethics in Accounting and Finance unit of the AAT Level 3 Diploma. This guide includes detail on the topics covered within the unit, and the depth and breadth to which these topics need to be taught and learnt.

The purpose of the unit

This knowledge unit recognises the importance of the ethical duties of an accounting technician. Its purpose is to support learners in:

- Working within AAT's Code of Professional Ethics, and other codes

- Promoting public confidence in accountancy practices or functions

- Enhancing the professional reputation and integrity of the learner and their organisation

Learning objectives

In the Professional Ethics in Accounting and Finance unit, learners develop an understanding of the importance of fulfilling the ethical duties that they have as accounting technicians. This involves recognising not only the rules with which they must comply, but also the principles on which these rules are based. Behaving ethically, and knowing when to take action on suspicions or knowledge of unethical behaviour and non-compliance with laws and regulations, protects the professional reputation of accounting technicians, their organisations, AAT and the accountancy profession as a whole. The result should be the continuing confidence of the public in accountants to protect the public interest. Learners therefore need to know what it means to behave ethically and also what to do if they become aware of any ethical issues in their environment.

Learning outcomes

This unit consists of three learning outcomes:

1. Understand the principles of ethical working in accountancy or payroll.

2. Know how to behave in an ethical manner when working with internal and external customers.

3. Understand when and how to take appropriate action following any suspected breaches of ethical codes.

QCF Unit	Learning Outcome	Assessment Criteria	Covered in Chapter
Professional Ethics in Accounting and Finance	**Understand the principles of ethical working in accountancy or payroll**	Explain the principles of ethical behaviour including integrity (including honesty), objectivity, professional and technical competence and due care, confidentiality, professional behaviour	1
		Summarise the relevant legal, regulatory and ethical requirements affecting the accounting and finance sector and your own industry	1
		Explain the role of professional bodies relevant to your work	1
		Explain why you, your organisation or industry are expected to operate within codes of conduct and practice	1
		Explain how organisations can be at risk from improper practice and why it is important to be vigilant	1 & 2
		Identify opportunities to maintain your continuing professional development in line with the requirements of relevant professional bodies	1

BPP LEARNING MEDIA

QCF Unit	Learning Outcome	Assessment Criteria	Covered in Chapter
	Know how to behave in an ethical manner when working with internal and external customers	Explain how to act appropriately and with integrity, honesty, fairness and sensitivity when working with clients, suppliers, colleagues and others	2
		Identify why it is important to keep a professional distance between professional duties and personal life at all times	2,3
		Explain why it is important to adhere to organisational and professional values, codes of practice and regulations at all times	1
		Explain why it is important to adhere to policies for handling clients' monies	3
		Explain why information should be kept confidential	1 & 3
		Identify circumstances when confidential information should be disclosed and who is entitled to the information	1 & 3
		Explain the importance of working within the limits and confines of your own professional experience, knowledge and expertise	3
		Summarise the advice to clients on the retention of books, working papers and other documents	3

QCF Unit	Learning Outcome	Assessment Criteria	Covered in Chapter
	Understand when and how to take appropriate action following suspected breaches of ethical codes	Identify the relevant authorities and internal departments to whom unethical behaviour, breaches of confidentiality, suspected illegal acts or other malpractice should be reported	4
		Recognise when the relevant authority should be advised if an employee has concerns over work they have been asked to complete	4
		Identify any inappropriate client behaviour and how to report it to the relevant authority	4
		Explain the procedures which should be followed if an employee suspects an employer, colleague or client has committed, or may commit, an act which is believed to be illegal or unethical eg whistle blowing	1 & 4

Delivery guidance

When teaching this unit tutors must stress the relevance and value of all three learning outcomes to all learners. Learners should be encouraged to become very familiar with AAT's Code of Professional Ethics over the course of delivery of the unit, and should be aware of the particular issues referred to in the Code.

1. Understand the principles of ethical working in accountancy or payroll

1.1 <u>Explain the principles of ethical behaviour including integrity (including honesty), objectivity, professional and technical competence and due care, confidentiality, professional behaviour</u>

 ▪ State the fundamental principles as set out in Part A AAT Code of Professional Ethics ss100 - 150:

BPP LEARNING MEDIA

- Integrity
- Objectivity
- Professional competence and due care
- Confidentiality
- Professional behaviour

■ State the types of threat to fundamental principles and safeguards against them as set out in ss100.12 – s100.17 AAT Code of Professional Ethics

■ Specify how the conceptual framework of threats and safeguards is designed to operate

1.2 <u>Summarise the relevant legal, regulatory and ethical requirements affecting the accounting and finance sector and your own industry</u>

■ Identify the importance of compliance with the law (civil and criminal), with other regulations and with ethical codes

■ State the legal status of the AAT's Code of Professional Ethics and its application to members in practice (Part B s200) and members in business (Part C s300)

    – State that members are held to account by AAT for breaches of its Code of Professional Ethics (eg students sign a declaration on their application for student membership agreeing to abide by the relevant regulations and policies of AAT)

    – Identify that AAT's Code of Professional Ethics interacts with other AAT policies and regulations, namely: Guidelines and Regulations for Members in Practice, AAT Memorandum and Articles of Association; Disciplinary Regulations; CPD Policy

■ Identify the limits of the Code in certain circumstances and the other regulations that may apply, for example that 'holding clients' money when running an investment business is subject to detailed FSA rules" (s270)

■ State the objectives of the accountancy profession (AAT Code of Professional Ethics 1.14)

■ Identify in outline the methods by which the accountancy and finance profession is regulated, for example the role of the FRC and its constituent boards in the UK

■ Identify the distinction in accountancy and finance between statutory regulated functions (the 'reserved areas' of audit, investment business and insolvency, see s200.4) and other functions (accounting and tax)

- Identify that other forms of regulation affecting the accountancy and finance sector as a whole: employment protection and equality laws, health and safety regulations and environmental regulations

- Identify other methods of regulating industries eg self-regulation, independent watchdogs, ombudsmen and government regulation

- Specify the basics of business ethics (in addition to professional ethics) eg codes of principles and values that govern decisions and actions within an organisation including:

  - The simple ethical test for a business decision from the Institute of Business Ethics: transparency, effect, fairness

  - The impact of the 'tone at the top' on corporate culture

1.3 Explain the role of professional bodies relevant to your work

- Specify the nature and role of, and relationship between, professional bodies that are relevant to their work, including AAT, sponsoring bodies of AAT, the CCAB and its member bodies, and IFAC

- Identify IFAC's International Ethics Standards Board for Accountants (IESBA) as the body setting global ethical standards for accountants

- Identify the nature and role of industry-related bodies eg HMRC, SOCA, the FSA

1.4 Explain why you, your organisation or industry are expected to operate within codes of conduct and practice

- State the legal status of codes of conduct and codes of practice in general, including industry or organisation-specific ethical codes

- State the objectives and functions of codes of conduct/codes of practice

- Identify the reasons why individuals, organisations and industries should operate within such codes

- Identify differences between a principles-based approach and a rules-based approach

1.5 Explain how organisations can be at risk from improper practice and why it is important to be vigilant

- Identify an appropriate definition of operational risk and factors which give rise to such risk, eg the Basel Committee on Banking Supervision definition

- Specify types of operational risk that arise from improper practice, eg process, people, systems and legal risks, and event risks (physical, social, political and economic events)

BPP
LEARNING MEDIA

- State the basic Money Laundering Regulations thresholds (s210.3) and procedures for customer due diligence (see Appendix)

- State the basic requirement on organisations to comply with the Bribery Act and possible consequences for non-compliance

1.6 Identify opportunities to maintain your continuing professional development in line with the requirements of relevant professional bodies

- Identify their obligations in relation to CPD including the CPD Cycle (AAT Code of Professional Ethics ss1.14, 100.5, 100.14, 130.3 and 200.3)

- Identify how AAT monitors members' compliance with CPD obligations

2. Know how to behave in an ethical manner when working with internal and external customers

2.1 Explain how to act appropriately and with integrity, honesty, fairness and sensitivity when working with clients, suppliers, colleagues and others

- Identify descriptions of behaviour that demonstrate integrity, honesty, fairness and sensitivity (including Part C AAT Code of Professional Ethics s320)

- Specify circumstances in which ethical behaviour is required (when liaising with clients, suppliers, colleagues and others)

- Identify behaviour that is both ethical and appropriate in a given set of circumstances, and behaviour that is unethical and inappropriate

- Identify how safeguards are used to address threats to the fundamental principles in a given set of circumstances (Part A AAT Code of Professional Ethics ss100-150, Part B AAT Code of Professional Ethics s200, Part C AAT Code of Professional Ethics s300) and what to do when a threat cannot be reduced to an acceptable level

- State the relevant provisions of the AAT Code of Professional Ethics in relation to professional appointment (s210), conflicts of interest (s220), second opinions (s230), fees and other types of remuneration (s240), marketing professional services (s250)

- State the Bribery Act offences for individuals and the penalties

2.2 Identify why it is important to keep a professional distance between professional duties and personal life at all times

- State what should be done about threats associated with lack of professional distance (including Part B AAT Code of Professional Ethics [conflicts of interest s220] and Part C AAT Code of Professional Ethics [financial interests s340])

- State the appropriate guidance on maintaining objectivity in Part B AAT Code of Professional Ethics s280

- State the appropriate guidance on gifts and hospitality for a member in practice (Part B AAT Code of Professional Ethics s260) and on inducements for a member in business (Part C AAT Code of Professional Ethics s350)

- State what is meant by 'independence' and the appropriate guidance on independence in a review and assurance engagement (Part B AAT Code of Professional Ethics s290.1 – s290.8)

2.3 Explain why it is important to adhere to organisational and professional values, codes of practice and regulations at all times

- Identify key organisational values (i.e. complying with regulations in spirit as well as to the letter with regard to: being transparent with customers; reporting financial and regulatory information; accepting and giving gifts and hospitality; paying suppliers a fair price and on time; providing fair treatment, decent wages and good working conditions to employees)

- Identify key professional values (including the fundamental principles and the additional relevant Nolan principles of accountability, openness and honesty)

- Specify the effect of codes of practice and regulations on organisations and individuals

- Specify the consequences of non-compliance with codes and regulations including disciplinary action (knowledge of the stages of the disciplinary process, and sections 7 to 13, in AAT's *Disciplinary Regulations for Members* is required)

2.4 Explain why it is important to adhere to policies for handling clients' monies

- State appropriate policies for handling clients' money (Part B AAT Code of Professional Ethics s 270)

- Identify the rules that members in practice are required to abide by in managing client monies in addition to s270 (see Appendix)

- Specify potential consequences of non-compliance with policies: money laundering (see Appendix), breach of investment business rules, fraud (Fraud Act 2006 offences)

2.5 Explain why information should be kept confidential

- Specify the importance of confidentiality, including both the fundamental principle (Part A AAT Code of Professional Ethics s 140.1 - 140.6) and legal rules (Data Protection Act 1998 and the role of the Information Commissioner's Office)

2.6 <u>Identify circumstances when confidential information should be disclosed and who is entitled to the information</u>

- Specify the disclosure provisions and matters to consider in deciding whether to disclose (Part A AAT Code of Professional Ethics s140.7 - 140.8)

- Identify from a given set of circumstances the appropriate course of action regarding disclosure

- Identify in a given set of circumstances the appropriate person/organisation to whom disclosure should be made (see Appendix)

2.7 <u>Explain the importance of working within the limits and confines of your own professional experience, knowledge and expertise</u>

- State the importance of working within their professional experience, knowledge and expertise, including an outline of contractual relationships, professional negligence and the Fraud Act 2006 offences

- Identify the broad issues regarding breach of contract in the supply of services by members in practice

- State the guidance on acting with sufficient expertise for a member in business (Part C AAT Code of Professional Ethics s330)

- Identify the appropriate response to requests for them to work outside the confines of their own professional experience and expertise in a given set of circumstances

2.8 <u>Summarise the advice to clients on the retention of books, working papers and other documents</u>

- State AAT guidance on ownership of books and records and retention of books, working papers and other documents (see Appendix)

- State the HMRC guidance on retention of accounting information

- State the requirements for keeping records in the context of the Money Laundering Regulations (see Appendix)

3. Understand when and how to take appropriate action following suspected breaches of ethical codes

3.1 <u>Identify the relevant authorities and internal departments to whom unethical behaviour, breaches of confidentiality, suspected illegal acts or other malpractice should be reported</u>

- Identify the money laundering/terrorist financing offences and their consequences (see Appendix)

- Identify the relevant authority to which reports should be made namely:

- Money Laundering Reporting Officer (MLRO) or Serious Organised Crime Agency (SOCA) regarding money laundering (see Appendix)

- MLRO/SOCA regarding tax errors/omissions (Part B AAT Code of Professional Ethics s160)

- Other relevant authorities in the UK and elsewhere (eg police if suspected fraud)

- Identify the prescribed internal or external department and/or professional body to which reports should be made regarding breach of codes of conduct/practice or AAT Code of Professional Ethics

3.2 <u>Recognise when the relevant authority should be advised if an employee has concerns over work they have been asked to complete</u>

- Specify the type of concern that may arise for an AAT member in business about work they have been asked to complete (Part C AAT Code of Professional Ethics s 310)

- Identify from a set of circumstances the appropriate time at which advice about concerns should be sought from the AAT Ethics Advice Line or employer-run service

3.3 <u>Identify any inappropriate client behaviour and how to report it to the relevant authority</u>

- Specify the type of concern that may arise for a member in practice about inappropriate client behaviour, including the potential for the offences of 'tipping off', 'failure to disclose' and 'prejudicing an investigation' (see Appendix)

- Specify the key threats to the fundamental principles that arise for a member in practice from inappropriate client behavior (familiarity, intimidation and advocacy threats) and the safeguards which could be in place to mitigate them

- Identify from a set of circumstances when and how advice about inappropriate client behaviour should be sought from the AAT Ethics Advice Line

- State how to report inappropriate client behaviour

BPP
LEARNING MEDIA

3.4 <u>Explain the procedures which should be followed if an employee suspects an employer, colleague or client has committed, or may commit, an act which is believed to be illegal or unethical eg whistle blowing</u>

- State the rules on members making required disclosures in either internal reports or suspicious activities reports regarding money laundering under the Proceeds of Crime Act 2002 and money laundering regulations (AAT Code of Professional Ethics s100.22, 140.7,and s210.4) (see Appendix)

- State the protection available for protected disclosures and authorised disclosures under these rules (see Appendix)

- Identify the protection available for 'whistle-blowers' under the Public Interest Disclosure Act 1998

APPENDIX TO UNIT GUIDANCE FOR PROFESSIONAL ETHICS IN ACCOUNTING AND FINANCE (PEAF)

Contents

Money laundering
Books and records
Managing client monies
AAT monitoring of compliance with CPD requirements

MONEY LAUNDERING

What are money laundering and terrorist financing?

Money laundering involves the proceeds of crime while terrorist financing may involve both legitimate property and the proceeds of crime.

Money laundering is the process by which criminally obtained money or other assets (criminal property) are exchanged for 'clean' money or other assets with no obvious link to their criminal origins. It also covers money, however come by, which is used to fund terrorism.

Criminal property is property which was obtained as a result of criminal conduct and the person knows or suspects that it was obtained from such conduct. It may take any form, including money or money's worth, securities, tangible property and intangible property.

Activities related to money laundering include:

- Acquiring, using or possessing criminal property

- Handling the proceeds of crimes such as theft, fraud and tax evasion

- Being knowingly involved in any way with criminal or terrorist property

- Entering into arrangements to facilitate laundering criminal or terrorist property

- Investing the proceeds of crimes in other financial products

- Investing the proceeds of crimes through the acquisition of property/assets

- Transferring criminal property.

Terrorist financing is fund raising, possessing or dealing with property or facilitating someone else to do so, when intending, knowing or suspecting or having reasonable cause to suspect that it is intended for the purposes of terrorism.

Terrorist property is money or property likely to be used for terrorist purposes or the proceeds of commissioning or carrying out terrorist acts.

What are the money laundering and terrorist financing offences?

The statutory definition of money laundering is 'an act which constitutes an offence under sections 327, 328 or 329 of POCA'.

These three money laundering offences are:

- s327 – Concealing, disguising, converting, transferring or removing criminal property.

- s328 – Taking part in an arrangement to facilitate the acquisition, use or control of criminal property.

- s329 – Acquiring, using or possessing criminal property.

Terrorism is the use or threat of action designed to influence government, or to intimidate any section of the public, or to advance a political, religious or ideological cause where the action would involve violence, threats to health and safety, damage to property or disruption of electronic systems.

The definition of 'terrorist property' means that all dealings with funds or property which are likely to be used for the purposes of terrorism, even if the funds are 'clean' in origin, is a terrorist financing offence.

There are no 'de minimis' exceptions in relation to either money laundering or terrorist financing offences.

Defences available to any person involved in money laundering offences and/or similar offences under TA 2000 include making an 'authorised disclosure' to the appropriate authorities.

The maximum penalty for money laundering or terrorist financing is 14 years imprisonment or an unlimited fine.

The UK legislation on money laundering and terrorist financing applies to the proceeds of conduct that is a criminal offence in the UK and most conduct occurring elsewhere that would have been an offence if it had taken place in the UK.

UK Anti-Money Laundering Legislation (AMLL)

The AMLL consist of:

- The Proceeds of Crime Act 2002 as amended (POCA)

- The Terrorism Act 2000 as amended (TA)

- Money Laundering Regulations 2007 (MLR)

To whom does the AMLL apply?

The three money laundering offences under POCA and the similar offences under TA can be committed by **any person.**

However POCA and TA include additional offences which can be committed by **individuals working in the regulated sector,** that is by people providing specified professional services such as accountancy. This means that an **accountant** (ie an AAT member in practice) will be personally liable for breaching POCA and TA if he or she provides accountancy services while turning a 'blind eye' to a client's suspect dealings.

The MLR impose duties on 'relevant persons' (sole traders and firms (not employees) operating within the regulated sector) to establish and maintain practice, policies and procedures to detect and deter activities relating to money laundering and terrorist financing. It is the sole trader or firm which will be liable therefore for any breach of the MLR.

The practice, policies and procedures required by the MLR of accountants include:

- Customer due diligence on clients

- Reporting money laundering/terrorist financing

- Record keeping

Customer due diligence (CDD) on clients

Timing of CDD

CDD must be applied by accountants to all new clients **before** services are provided to them and at appropriate times to existing clients on a risk-sensitive basis.

The one exception to this is where to do so would interrupt the normal conduct of business and there is little risk of money laundering or terrorist financing, in which case the accountant must always:

- Find out who the client claims to be before commencing the client's instructions and

- Complete CDD as soon as reasonably possible afterwards.

MLR state that CDD must be applied in the following situations:

- When establishing a business relationship

- When carrying out an occasional transaction (i.e. involving 15,000 euro or the equivalent in sterling or more)

- Where there is a suspicion of money laundering or terrorist financing or

- Where there are doubts about previously obtained customer identification information.

Elements of CDD for new clients

There are three elements to CDD for new clients:

1. Find out who the client claims to be – name, address, date of birth – and obtain evidence to check that the client is as claimed.

2. Obtain evidence so the accountant is satisfied that he or she knows who any beneficial owners are. This means beneficial owners must be considered on an individual basis. Generally, a beneficial owner is an individual who ultimately owns 25% or more of the client or the transaction property.

3. Obtain information on the purpose and intended nature of the transaction.

The evidence obtained can be documentary, data or information from a reliable and independent source, or a mix of all of these.

If CDD cannot be completed, **the accountant must not act for the client** - and should consider whether to submit an Internal Report or Suspicious Activity Report, as appropriate (see below).

On-going monitoring of existing clients

On-going monitoring must be applied to existing clients. This means that an accountant must:

▪   Carry out appropriate and risk-sensitive CDD measures to any transaction which appears to be inconsistent with knowledge of the client or the client's business or risk profile. For example, if a client suddenly has an injection of significant funds, check the source of funds. If a beneficial owner is revealed, obtain evidence of the beneficial owner's identity and the nature and purpose of the injection of the funds.

▪   Keep CDD documents, data and information up to date. For example, if a client company has a change to its directorship, update records accordingly.

Reporting money laundering/terrorist financing

Accountant's duty to report

POCA and TA impose an obligation on accountants (individuals within the regulated sector, including those involved in providing accountancy services to clients ie AAT members in practice), to submit in defined circumstances:

1. An Internal Report to a Money Laundering Reporting Officer (MLRO), by those employed in a group practice

2. A Suspicious Activity Report (SAR) to the Serious Organised Crime Agency (SOCA), by sole practitioners and MLROs.

There are two circumstances (subject to exceptions, below) when a required disclosure in an internal report or a SAR, collectively referred to below as a report, must be made by an accountant:

1. When the accountant wishes to provide services in relation to property which it is actually known or suspected relates to money laundering or terrorist financing. In such circumstances, the reporter must indicate in the report that consent is required to provide such services, and must refrain from doing so until consent is received.

2. When the accountant actually knows or suspects, or there are reasonable (objective) grounds for knowing or suspecting, that another person is engaged in money laundering or terrorist financing, whether or not he or she wishes to act for such person. The person in question could be a client, a colleague or a third party.

'Failure to disclose' offence for accountants

It is an offence for an accountant to fail to disclose a suspicion or knowledge of money laundering.

The maximum penalty for failure to disclose is 5 years imprisonment or an unlimited fine.

Exceptions to the duty to report

The obligation of an accountant to report does NOT apply if:

1. The information which forms the basis of knowledge or suspicion or the reasonable grounds to know or suspect was obtained other than in the course of the accountant's business, for example, on a social occasion.

2. The information came about in privileged circumstances, that is in order for the accountant to provide legal advice, such as explaining a client's tax liability (except when it is judged that the advice has been sought to enable the client to commit a criminal offence or avoid detection) or expert opinion or services in relation to actual or contemplated legal proceedings.

3. There is a reasonable excuse for not reporting, in which case the report must be made as soon as reasonable in the circumstances.

Contents of the report: required disclosure

The internal report or SAR must contain, at a minimum, the required disclosure of:

- The identity of the suspect (if known),

BPP
LEARNING MEDIA

- The information or other matter on which the knowledge or suspicion of money laundering (or reasonable grounds for such) is based and

- The whereabouts of the laundered property (if known).

Reports made under POCA are either protected disclosures or authorised disclosures.

Effect of a report: protected disclosure

Any report providing the required disclosure which is made by **any** person, not just an accountant, forming a money laundering suspicion, at work or when carrying out professional activities (whether or not providing accountancy services to clients), is a protected disclosure. This means the person is protected against allegations of breach of confidentiality, however the restriction on disclosure of information was imposed.

Note: any individual, business or organisation may make a voluntary protected disclosure; it is only in the regulated sector that such reports are compulsory.

Effect of a report: authorised disclosure

Any person who realises they may have engaged in or be about to engage in money laundering should make what is known as an authorised disclosure to the appropriate authority. This may provide a defence against charges of money laundering provided it is made before the act is carried out (and SOCA's consent to the act is obtained), or it is made as soon as possible on the initiative of that person after the act is done and with good reason being shown for the delay (eg the person did not realise criminal property was involved and made the report on their own initiative as soon as this was suspected/known).

'Tipping off' offence for accountants

Once an accountant has made a report, or has become aware that a report has been made*, a criminal offence is committed if information is disclosed that is likely to prejudice any actual or contemplated investigation following the report. The person making the disclosure does not have to intend to prejudice an investigation for this offence to apply.

*Note: the report does not have to have been made by the person making the tip-off; that person merely needs to know or suspect that one has been made to a MLRO, SOCA, HMRC or the police.

The maximum penalty for tipping off is 5 years imprisonment or an unlimited fine.

'Prejudicing an investigation' offence for all persons

An offence may be committed where **any** person (not just an accountant):

- Knows or suspects that a money laundering investigation is being conducted or is about to be conducted; and

- Makes a disclosure which is likely to prejudice the investigation; or

- Falsifies, conceals or destroys documents relevant to the investigation, or causes that to happen.

The person making the disclosure does not have to intend to prejudice an investigation for this offence to apply. However, there is a defence available if the person making the disclosure did not know or suspect the disclosure would be prejudicial, did not know or suspect the documents were relevant, or did not intend to conceal any facts from the person carrying out the investigation.

Record keeping

Under the MLR, records should be maintained to assist any future law enforcement investigation relating to clients, and to demonstrate that the accountant has complied with statutory obligations. Such records should include:

- Copies of or reference to the CDD identification evidence (see below). These records must be kept for 5 years starting with the date on which the accountant's relationship with the client ends

- Copies or originals of documents relating to transactions that have been subject to CCD measures or ongoing monitoring. These must be kept for 5 years starting with the date on which the accountant completed the client's instructions

BOOKS AND RECORDS

Ownership of books and records

The rules concerning the ownership of books and records as between a client and an accountant engaged by the client to perform agreed services derive mainly from a combination of statute law and case law. It is important that the accountant is familiar with local laws and the following relates only to the position under English laws. The following paragraphs summarise the principal points on which guidance may be required. Before entering into contracts with clients an accountant must ensure that they are familiar with the local legal position and take steps to ensure that the engagement letter covers, as far as reasonably possible, the respective rights and responsibilities of both parties.

Generally where an accountant does not own the documents and records created in the course of acting for a client, they will be deemed to belong to the client. When determining the question of ownership of the documents, the following considerations are relevant:

1. The nature of the agreement with the client as evidenced in an engagement letter

2. The capacity in which the accountant acts in relation to the client (i.e. as principal or agent)

3. The purpose for which the documents and records exist or are brought into being

As a general rule, under English law:

- Where an accountant is acting as a principal (and not as an agent) in relation to the client, only documents brought into being on the specific instructions of the client belong to the client. Documents which are prepared, acquired or brought into being solely for the accountant's own purpose as a principal belong to the accountant.

- Where the accountant is acting as an agent, any documents will generally be the property of the client.

Examples:

- Accounting records and financial statements prepared for a client belong, under UK law, to the client. The working papers belong to the accountant.

- In taxation work, documents such as tax correspondence (letters and copies of letters to a third party) will normally belong to the client.

- Where tax, investment or other advice is given to a client, the written advice, including supporting papers, belong to the client, but the working papers belong to the accountant.

- Letters received from the client, copies of letters from the accountant to the client and notes made of discussions with the client belong to the accountant.

- Ownership of copies of communications between the accountant and third parties depends on the relationship with the client. The guidance above will generally apply to such communications.

Retention of books, working papers and other documents

There are many reasons why an accountant may want to retain client books, working papers and other documents. The most important of these are to ensure that information is accessible when necessary to:

- Assist a tax investigation by the tax authorities, or

- Defend a complaint or negligence claim brought by a disaffected client.

The law on professional negligence requires that persons with a legitimate cause should make their claim within a reasonable time. A number of statutes lay down specific periods of time within which actions must be commenced. However,

where statutes do not specify time limits, the Limitation Act 1980 and any successor legislation sets out the general position on time limits. For professionals who may be engaged in contractual disputes books, working papers and other documents should be retained for the period of limitation set out in the Act, that is, no less than 6 years.

Since a disaffected client or other person could issue a writ against the accountant before the end of the expiry of the six year period, and delay serving it for up to a year, 7 years might, in fact, be the most prudent retention period.

In any event, taxation records should be retained for 7 years from the end of the engagement.

It is important to note that there may be significant differences between English law and the law of other countries where the time limits quoted above will not necessarily apply. If in doubt about the time limits applicable to the retention of books, working papers or other documents, the accountant should consult a legal adviser.

There is no specific format on how to retain books, working papers or other documents. As practice size grows, the accountant may find that it is not practical to keep actual paper files and electronic storage may offer a better alternative. However, when deciding how to store documents, it is important to be aware of responsibilities created under the Data Protection Act 1998 and ensure these are not breached.

Lien over documents

Under English law, a professional will generally have a right to exercise a particular lien over documents in situations where work has been carried out on those documents for a client and the bill rendered has not been paid. This means that the accountant will have a right to retain possession of the documents until fees have been paid for the work carried out in relation to those documents.

The right of lien is a common law remedy which the courts have developed over the years. There are rules that apply to certain types of document and conditions to be met before the right can be properly exercised. A right of lien will exist only when the following conditions are met:

1.   The documents retained are the property of the client and not of a third party

2.   The documents have come into the accountant's possession by proper means, and work has been done by the accountant on the documents. This prohibits the exercise of a general right of lien

3.   The accountant has rendered an adequately detailed fee note and the fees are outstanding in respect of that work

An accountant is not able to exercise a lien in respect of documents of the same client on which past remunerated work was carried out. Similarly, where fees are outstanding on the part of a company, a member cannot exercise a lien on the documents which are the personal property of a director of such company.

Further, special rules apply in relation to the statutory books and accounting records of companies, and where documents are claimed by an administrator or liquidator of a company, or the Official Receiver or a Trustee in Bankruptcy. A right of lien cannot be asserted over statutory books or documents of a registered company which the company is obliged to have available for public inspection or to be kept at the registered office or some other specified place. Documents such as the register of members, and the directors' minute books, cannot become the subject of a lien.

Similarly, a right of lien cannot be exercised over accounting records of a registered company as such records are required to be open for inspection under the Companies Act 2006. Examples of such records include purchase invoices, cheque books, paying-in-books and bank statements. If in doubt about whether particular documents constitute accounting records, the accountant should seek independent advice.

A right of lien cannot be exercised over administrative records of a company that is subject to an administration order, is in liquidation or has appointed a provisional liquidator where the liquidator is unable to obtain possession of such records in any other way. The exception to this is where the documents give title to property (for example, title deeds, share certificates or bills of lading) or have been pledged or are held as security for some liability of the company and are held on that basis.

Similarly, the law does not permit the exercise of a lien over any records of a bankrupt person except where the exception above applies.

Due to the complex nature of this area, it is important that legal advice should be sought on the exceptions and how they may affect the right of lien. Before deciding to exercise the right, it is important to carefully consider other legal options for collecting unpaid fees for example; action at small claims court, debt collection agencies etc. Whatever method is decided on, it is important that it is in accordance with the fundamental principles of professional ethics, particularly as it relates to professional behaviour.

MANAGING CLIENT MONIES

Regulation 24 of the Regulations for Members in Practice sets out the rules AAT members in practice (MiPs) have to follow when dealing with client monies. MiPs are prohibited from holding monies related to investments unless they are authorised to do so under the Financial Services and Markets Act 2000.

What are client monies?

Client monies are any funds, or form of documents of title to money, or documents of title which can be converted into money that an MiP holds on behalf of his or her client. This does not include any sum that is immediately due and payable on demand, for example the MiP's fees for work done or fees paid in advance for work to be done.

Client monies do not include the use and control of a client's own bank account. However, where an MiP has control of the client's own bank account, the client's specific written authority must have been obtained and acknowledged by the client's bank before the MiP exercises any control over such bank account and adequate records of the transactions undertaken must be maintained.

Examples of items that will normally constitute client monies include:

- HMRC refunds received on behalf of clients

- Funds entrusted to an MiP by the client to assist in carrying out the client's instructions

- Surplus funds that fall at the end of an engagement.

How and when to hold client monies

Where an MiP holds client monies, such monies are held in trust and the accountant is acting as a trustee and must be prepared to account to the client upon request. Failure to properly account could result in criminal and/or civil proceedings for theft and/or abuse of position.

Client monies cannot be held in certain circumstances, including:

- Where the MiP knows or suspects the monies represent criminal property or are to be used for illegal activities

- Where there is no justification for holding the monies, for example the monies do not relate to a service the MiP provides.

- Where a condition on the MiP's licence or registration prohibits dealing with client monies.

The following are conditions that apply when a MiP holds client monies:

- The monies must be kept separately from personal monies or monies belonging to the MiP's practice

- The monies must only be used for the purpose for which they were intended.

- The monies must be held in the same currency that it was received unless the client has given instructions to exchange into another currency

- The MiP must ensure that the client has been identified and verified on a risk-sensitive basis before holding monies on their behalf

- The MiP must be ready at all times to account for those monies or any income, dividends or gains generated on them, to the client or any persons entitled to such accounting.

AAT MONITORING OF COMPLIANCE WITH CPD REQUIREMENTS

All AAT full and fellow members must comply with AAT's CPD policy, go through the CPD cycle at least once in a 12 month period (twice in the case of a MiP) and keep adequate CPD records.

If an AAT member fails to comply with AAT's CPD policy, AAT may take disciplinary action. This could ultimately result in the member's expulsion from AAT.

The intention of AAT, however, is to help members with their professional development so that this situation does not arise.

AAT conducts regular monitoring programmes twice a year involving checking CPD compliance of a sample of full and fellow AAT members. These members are selected for these programmes both randomly and on the basis of risk.

The onus is on the member to demonstrate to AAT's satisfaction that he or she complies with AAT's CPD policy. If AAT does not feel a member's CPD records provide confirmation of his or her compliance with AAT policy, it will provide guidance on how to approach CPD in the future.

Cases of persistent and wilful non-compliance will be subject to disciplinary proceedings in line with AAT's Disciplinary Regulations.

chapter 1:
THE PRINCIPLES OF ETHICAL WORKING

chapter coverage 📖

In this opening chapter, we consider the fundamental principles of ethical behaviour as they apply in the general context of the UK accountancy profession, and the framework set out by the AAT's *Code of Professional Ethics* and the regulatory environment.

We consider the role of the main professional bodies relevant to your work, the importance of codes of conduct and codes of practice in business dealings, and the importance of maintaining your continuing professional development.

The topics we cover are:

- ✍ What are ethics?
- ✍ Why behave ethically?
- ✍ Fundamental ethical principles
- ✍ The conceptual framework
- ✍ Principles versus rules
- ✍ Compliance with the law
- ✍ The accountancy profession
- ✍ Codes of conduct and codes of practice
- ✍ Business ethics and professional values
- ✍ Risks from improper practice
- ✍ AAT disciplinary regulations
- ✍ Continuing professional development (CPD)

WHAT ARE ETHICS?

Ethics are a set of moral principles that guide behaviour.

Ethical values are assumptions and beliefs about what constitutes 'right' and 'wrong' behaviour.

Individuals have ethical values, often reflecting the beliefs of the families, cultures and educational environments in which they developed their ideas.

Organisations also have ethical values, based on the norms and standards of behaviour that their leaders believe will best help them express their identity and achieve their objectives.

The concept of **business ethics** suggests that businesses are morally responsible for their actions, and should be held accountable for the effects of their actions on people and society. This is true for individual businesses (which should behave ethically towards the employees, customers, suppliers and communities who are affected by them) and for 'business' in general, which has a duty to behave responsibly in the interests of the society of which it is a part.

Some of these ethical values may be explicit: included in the organisation's mission statement, set out in ethical codes and guidelines, or taught in employee training programmes. Other values may be part of the **organisation culture**: 'the way we do things around here', the unwritten rules and customs of behaviour that develop over time as people find ways of working together.

A **code of ethics** often focuses on social issues. It may set out general principles about an organisation's beliefs on matters such as mission, quality, privacy or the environment. The effectiveness of such codes of ethics depends on the extent to which management supports them 'from the top'. The code of ethics often gives rise to a **code of conduct** for employees.

Task 1

Think of some examples of the kinds of behaviour that you consider 'right' or 'wrong' in your personal and professional life.

BPP
LEARNING MEDIA

WHY BEHAVE ETHICALLY?

The AAT has a **Code of Professional Ethics** (the AAT Code) in place, which came into effect on 1 September 2011. This replaces the previous AAT Guidelines on Professional Ethics. The AAT Code is based on the **Code of Ethics for Professional Accountants** produced by the International Ethics Standards Board for Accountants (IESBA) of the International Federation of Accountants (IFAC). AAT is an associate member (not a full member or affiliate) of IFAC.

The AAT Code on which this text is substantially based notes that: 'the decisions you make in the everyday course of your professional lives can have real ethical implications.'

The AAT Code is in three parts:

- Part A 'General application of the code' applies to all members.

- Part B 'Members in practice' represents additional guidance which applies specifically to members in practice.

- Part C 'Members in business' applies specifically to members in business.

The AAT Code works in tandem with other AAT policies and regulations, such as the Guidelines and Regulations for Members in Practice, the AAT Memorandum and Articles of Association, AAT's Disciplinary Regulations, and AAT's CPD policy. We look at some of these in more detail later in this chapter.

The **objectives of the accountancy profession** are set out in the AAT Code in paragraph 1.14:

(i) The mastering of **particular skills and techniques** acquired through learning and education and maintained through continuing professional development

(ii) Development of an **ethical approach to work**, as well as to employers and clients. This is acquired by experience and professional supervision under training and is safeguarded by strict ethical and disciplinary guidelines

(iii) Acknowledgement of **duties to society** as a whole, in addition to duties to the employer or the client

(iv) An outlook which is essentially **objective**, obtained by being fair minded and free from conflicts of interest

(v) Rendering services to the **highest standards** of conduct and performance

(vi) Achieving **acceptance by the public** that members provide accountancy services in accordance with these high standards and requirements

The aim of the AAT Code is to help members achieve the above objectives. There are several key reasons why an accounting technician should strive to behave ethically:

- Ethical issues may be a matter of **law and regulation**. You are expected to know and apply the **civil and criminal law** of the country in which you live and work – as a basic minimum requirement for good practice. The AAT Code is based on the laws effective in the UK, with which members are expected to comply as a minimum requirement. (It is sometimes said that 'the law is a floor': the lowest acceptable level of behaviour required to preserve the public interest and individual rights.)

- The **AAT** (like other professional bodies) requires its members to conduct themselves, and provide services to clients, according to certain professional and ethical standards. It does this, in part, to maintain its own **reputation and standing** – but this is also of benefit to its members and to the accounting profession as a whole.

- Professional and ethical behaviour protects the **public interest**. The accountancy profession sees itself as having duties to society as a whole – in addition to its specific obligations to employers and clients.

The advice for AAT members, in a nutshell, is as follows:

- Completely avoid even the appearance of **conflict of interest**.

- Be **objective** and act in the **public interest,** because your responsibility is not exclusively to satisfy the needs of an individual client or employer.

- Keep sensitive information **confidential**. Accountants often deal with their employer's or client's most private material.

- Be **straightforward and honest** in professional and business relationships.

- Maintain **professional knowledge, behaviour and skills** at the level required by a client or employer.

- Act within the **spirit and the letter of the law** so as not to bring the profession into disrepute.

FUNDAMENTAL ETHICAL PRINCIPLES

You MUST print out a copy of the AAT's Code of Professional Ethics from the AAT's website (www.aat.org.uk) and refer to it as you work through the professional ethics unit.

You might have your own ideas about what 'ethical behaviour' looks like – and these ideas will be shaped by your personal assumptions and values, and the values of the culture in which you operate (at work and in the country in which you live). However, there are five **fundamental principles** set out in the AAT Code that underpin ethical behaviour in an accounting context:

Fundamental principle	Explanation	Section of AAT Code
Integrity	A member shall be straightforward and honest in all professional and business relationships.	110
Objectivity	A member shall not allow bias, conflict of interest or undue influence of others to override professional or business relationships.	120
Professional competence and due care	A member has a continuing duty to maintain professional knowledge and skill at the level required to ensure that a client or employer receives competent professional service based on current developments in practice, legislation and techniques. A member shall act diligently and in accordance with applicable and professional standards when providing professional services.	130
Confidentiality	A member shall, in accordance with the law, respect the confidentiality of information acquired as a result of professional and business relationships and not disclose any such information to third parties without proper and specific authority unless there is a legal or professional right or duty to disclose. Confidential information acquired as a result of professional and business relationships shall not be used for the personal advantage of the member or third parties.	140

Fundamental principle	Explanation	Section of AAT Code
Professional behaviour	A member shall comply with relevant laws and regulations and avoid any action that brings the profession into disrepute.	150

Let's look at each of these in turn.

Integrity – section 110

110.1 "The principle of **integrity** imposes an obligation on all members to be straightforward and honest in professional and business relationships. Integrity also implies fair dealing and truthfulness.

110.2 A member shall not be associated with reports, returns, communications or other information where they believe that the information:

(i) Contains a false or misleading statement

(ii) Contains statements or information furnished recklessly

(iii) Omits or obscures information required to be included where such omission or obscurity would be misleading."

On an everyday level, integrity involves matters such as being **open** about the limitations of your knowledge or competence, being **honest** in your relationships and carrying out your work **accurately, conscientiously and efficiently**.

Objectivity – section 120

120.1 "The principle of objectivity imposes an obligation on all members not to compromise their professional or business judgement because of bias, conflict of interest or the undue influence of others."

This is a very important principle for the accounting profession because it protects the interests both of the parties directly affected by an accountant's services and of the general public (who rely on the accuracy of information and the integrity of financial systems).

Objectivity is the principle that all professional and business judgements should be made fairly:

- On the basis of an **independent** and intellectually honest appraisal of information

- **Free from** all forms of **prejudice** and **bias**

BPP LEARNING MEDIA

- Free from factors which might affect **impartiality**, such as pressure from a superior, financial interest in the outcome, a personal or professional relationship with one of the parties involved, or a conflict of interest (where one client stands to lose and another to gain by a particular disclosure)

Task 2

A member who is straightforward and honest in all business and professional relationships can be said to be following the fundamental principle of objectivity.

	✓
True	
False	

Professional competence and due care – section 130

Accountants have an obligation to their employers and clients to know what they are doing – and to do it right! The following is taken from the AAT Code:

130.1 "The principle of **professional competence** and due care imposes the following obligations on members:

    (i)   To maintain **professional knowledge** and **skill** at the level required to ensure that clients or employers receive competent professional service and

    (ii)   To **act diligently** in accordance with applicable technical and professional standards when providing professional services.

130.2 Competent professional service requires the exercise of **sound judgement** in applying professional knowledge and skill in the performance of such service. Professional competence may be divided into two separate phases:

    (i)   Attainment of professional competence and

    (ii)   Maintenance of professional competence.

130.3 The **maintenance of professional competence** requires continuing awareness and understanding of relevant technical, professional and business developments. Continuing professional development (CPD) develops and maintains the capabilities that enable a member to perform competently within the professional environment. To achieve this, Council expects all members to undertake CPD in accordance with the AAT *Policy on continuing professional development*. This requires members to assess, plan, action and evaluate their learning and development needs.

130.4 **Diligence** encompasses the **responsibility** to act in accordance with the requirements of an assignment, carefully, thoroughly and on a timely basis.

130.5 A member shall take reasonable steps to ensure that those working under the member's authority in a **professional capacity** have appropriate **training** and **supervision**.

130.6 Where appropriate, a member shall make clients, employers or other users of the professional services aware of **limitations** inherent in the services to avoid the misinterpretation of an expression of opinion as an assertion of fact."

You should understand from this that you must not agree to carry out a task or assignment if you do not have the competence to carry it out to a **satisfactory standard** – unless you are sure that you will be able to get the help and advice you need to do so. And if you discover in the course of performing a task or assignment that you lack the knowledge or competence to complete it satisfactorily, you should not continue without taking steps to get the help you need.

In addition, once you have become a member of the profession, you need to maintain and develop your professional and **technical competence**, to keep pace with the demands which may be made on you in your work – and developments which may affect your work over time. This may mean:

- Regularly reviewing your practices against national and international standards, codes, regulations and legislation. Are you complying with the latest requirements?

- Continually upgrading your knowledge and skills in line with developments in accounting practices, requirements and techniques – and making sure that you do not get 'rusty' in the skills you have!

Task 3

Identify the appropriate word to use in the following sentence:

'Continuing professional development (CPD) is important to accountancy professionals as it helps them [▼] competency in their role.'

Picklist:

attain
maintain

Due care is a legal concept that means that, having agreed to do a task or assignment, you have an obligation to carry it out to the best of your ability, in the client's or employer's best interests, within reasonable timescales and with

BPP LEARNING MEDIA

proper regard for the technical and professional standards expected of you as a professional.

As the expert in your field, you may often deal with others who have little knowledge of accounting matters. This puts you in a position of power, which must never be abused by carrying out your task or assignment in a negligent or 'careless' way.

Confidentiality – section 140

140.1 "The principle of **confidentiality** imposes an obligation on members to refrain from:

(i) **Disclosing** outside the firm or employing organisation confidential information acquired as a result of professional and business relationships without proper and specific authority or unless there is a legal or professional right or duty to disclose and

(ii) **Using confidential information** acquired as a result of professional and business relationships to their personal advantage or the advantage of third parties.

Information about a past, present, or prospective client's or **employer's affairs**, or the affairs of clients of employers, acquired in a work context, is likely to be confidential if it is not a matter of public knowledge.

140.2 A member shall maintain confidentiality even in a **social environment.** The member shall be alert to the possibility of inadvertent disclosure, particularly in circumstances involving close or personal relations, associates and long established business relationships.

140.3 A member shall maintain confidentiality of information disclosed by a **prospective client** or **employer**.

140.4 A member shall maintain confidentiality of information within the firm or **employing organisation**.

140.5 A member shall take all **reasonable steps** to ensure that **staff under their control** and persons from whom advice and assistance is obtained **respect** the principle of **confidentiality**. The restriction on using confidential information also means not using it for any purpose other than that for which it was legitimately acquired.

140.6 The need to comply with the principle of confidentiality **continues even after the end of relationships** between a member and a client or employer. When a member changes employment or acquires a new client, the member is entitled to use prior experience. The member shall not, however, use or disclose any confidential information either acquired or received as a result of a professional or business relationship."

Confidentiality is a very important fundamental principle but there are circumstances where the law **allows or requires** that confidentiality to be breached. These circumstances are described in the AAT Code in section 140.7 and are summarised in the table below.

Circumstance	Examples
Disclosure is permitted by law and is authorised by the client or employer.	Providing working papers to a new firm who is taking on the client
Disclosure is required by law.	Providing documents or other evidence for legal proceedings
	Disclosure to HMRC
	Disclosure of actual/suspected money laundering or terrorist financing to the firm's Money Laundering Reporting Officer (MLRO) or to the Serious Organised Crime Agency (SOCA) (in the UK)
There is a professional right or duty to disclose which is in the public interest and is not prohibited by law.	Complying with the quality review of an IFAC member body or other professional body
	Responding to an inquiry or investigation by the AAT or other regulatory or professional body
	Disclosure to protect the member's professional interests in legal proceedings
	A disclosure made to comply with technical standards and ethics requirements

It is vital to appreciate the importance of the fundamental principle of **confidentiality**. You need to respect the confidentiality of information acquired as a result of professional and business relationships. This means that you will not use or disclose confidential information to others, unless:

- You have **specific** and **'proper' authorisation** to do so by the client or employer.

- You are legally or professionally **entitled** or *obliged* to do so.

It is also worth being aware that personal information shared with you by clients and colleagues at work should be regarded as confidential – unless you are told otherwise: this is an important basis for trust in any working relationship.

Task 4

In which of the following circumstances do you have a legal duty to disclose confidential information concerning a customer of your organisation?

	✓
If they are asked for during legal proceedings	
When your manager tells you to disclose the information	
When writing a report for general circulation within your organisation	

Professional behaviour – section 150

The final fundamental principle is professional behaviour. On this principle the AAT Code states:

> 150.1 "The principle of **professional behaviour** imposes an obligation on members to comply with relevant laws and regulations and avoid any action that may bring disrepute to the profession. This includes actions which a **reasonable and informed third party**, having knowledge of all relevant information, would conclude negatively affect the good reputation of the profession.
>
> Members should note that conduct reflecting adversely on the reputation of the AAT is a ground for disciplinary action under the AAT's *Disciplinary Regulations*."

An example is when advertising their services, members must ensure that they are honest and truthful. They can bring the profession into disrepute by making **exaggerated claims** about services, their qualifications and experience, or if they make **disparaging references or unsubstantiated comparisons** to the work of others.

Applying this principle means **'being professional'**. You'll have your own ideas about what 'being professional' means, but in a sense, it involves behaving in a way that maintains or enhances the reputation of your profession: bringing it credit – not discredit.

One key aspect of this is **courtesy**. As a professional, you should behave with courtesy and consideration towards anyone you come into contact with in the course of your work and indeed in your personal life.

> It is IMPOSSIBLE for us to overstate the importance of each of these fundamental principles – you MUST be able to recognise each of them.

HOW IT WORKS

Now that we've considered the fundamental principles in general, let's consider some typical scenarios in which they might be helpful. In each case, we will identify the ethical issues they present, in line with the basic principles discussed so far. For the purposes of these questions you should assume you are an AAT student.

Incident one

You are asked to produce an aged receivables' listing for your manager as soon as possible. However you do not have up to date figures because of a problem with the computer system. A colleague suggests that to get the report done in time you use averages for the missing figures.

There is an **integrity** issue here. Using averages instead of actual figures will almost certainly result in an inaccurate listing. You should report the problem to your manager and ask for an extension to your deadline in order to provide an accurate listing.

Incident two

You have received a letter from an estate agent, requesting financial information about one of your company's customers that is applying to rent a property. The information is needed as soon as possible, by fax or e-mail, in order to secure approval for the rent agreement.

There is a **confidentiality** issue here. You need the customer's authority to disclose the information; you may also need to confirm the identity of the person making the request. You should also take steps to protect the confidentiality of the information when you send it: for example, not using fax or e-mail (which can be intercepted), and stating clearly that the information is confidential.

Incident three

While out to lunch, you run into a friend at the sandwich bar. In conversation, she tells you that she expects to inherit from a recently deceased uncle, and asks you how she will be affected by inheritance tax, capital gains tax and other matters.

There are issues of **professional competence and due care** here. You are not qualified to give advice on matters of taxation. Even if you were qualified, any answer you give on the spot would risk being incomplete or inaccurate with potentially serious consequences.

BPP
LEARNING MEDIA

Incident four

A client of the accountancy practice you work in is so pleased with the service you gave him this year that he offers you a free weekend break in a luxury hotel, just as a 'thank you'.

There is an **objectivity** issue here as the gift is of significant value. Think about how it looks: a third party observer is entitled to wonder what 'special favours' deserve this extra reward – and/or how such a gift may bias you in the client's favour in future.

 Signpost

See the AAT Code of Professional Ethics:

- **Section 100**: Introduction and code of fundamental principles
- **Section 110**: Integrity
- **Section 120**: Objectivity
- **Section 130**: Professional competence and due care
- **Section 140**: Confidentiality
- **Section 150**: Professional behaviour

THE CONCEPTUAL FRAMEWORK

It is impossible to give guidelines on every possible situation that may arise in the course of your work which conflicts with the fundamental ethical principles. The AAT Code therefore sets out a basic **problem solving procedure,** which you can use in any situation, to give yourself the best chance of complying with the principles. This procedure forms the **'conceptual framework'** which requires the following:

- Identify where there may be a **threat** to a fundamental principle.

- **Evaluate the threat**: how significant is it?

- For any significant threat **apply safeguards** that will eliminate the threat or reduce it to an acceptable level (so that compliance with the fundamental principle is not compromised).

- If safeguards cannot be applied, **decline or discontinue** the specific action or professional service involved, or where necessary, **resign** from the client (if you are a member in practice) or the employing organisation (if you are a member in business).

We shall now look at threats and safeguards in more detail.

Threats

Many of the threats that may create a risk of compromising the fundamental principles will fall into one of the following five categories (section 100.12 of the AAT Code):

Threat	Explanation	Examples
Self-interest	Financial or other interests may inappropriately influence the member's judgement or behaviour	Undue fee dependence on one particular client
Self-review	A previous judgement needs to be re-evaluated by the member responsible for that judgement	Tax and accountancy work carried out by the same engagement team
Advocacy	A member promotes a position or opinion to the point that subsequent objectivity may be compromised	Acting on behalf of an assurance client which is in litigation or dispute with a third party
Familiarity	Due to close or personal relationships, a member becomes too sympathetic to the interests of others	A senior member undertaking an assurance engagement for a number of years for the same client
Intimidation	A member may be deterred from acting objectively by threats (actual or perceived)	Threatened withdrawal of services by a dominant client

Safeguards

The AAT Code defines safeguards as '**actions or other measures that may eliminate threats or reduce them to an acceptable level.**' The Code identifies two broad categories of safeguards that you might use to reduce or eliminate the threats we have described above (sections 100.13 and 100.14):

- **Safeguards created by the profession and/or legislation and regulation**. These include:

  - Education, training and experience, as requirements for entry into the profession

  - CPD

  - Corporate governance regulations

BPP LEARNING MEDIA

- – Professional standards
- – Professional or regulatory monitoring and disciplinary procedures
- – External review of financial reports, returns, communications or information produced by members
- **Safeguards in the work environment**, which increase the likelihood of identifying or deterring unethical behaviour, include:
  - – Quality controls, and internal audits of quality controls
  - – Mechanisms to empower and protect staff who raise ethical concerns ('whistleblowers')
  - – Involvement of, or consultation with, independent third parties (eg non executive directors or regulatory bodies)
  - – Rotation of personnel to avoid increasing familiarity and opportunities for collusion in fraud
  - – Opportunities to discuss ethical dilemmas (eg with an ethics officer, committee or forum)

Specific safeguards are considered in more detail in later chapters in terms of members in practice and members in business.

Task 5

Jake has been put under significant pressure by his manager to change the conclusion of a report he has written which reflects badly on the manager's performance.

Which threat is Jake facing?

	✓
Self-interest	
Advocacy	
Intimidation	

➡ Signpost

See the AAT Code of Professional Ethics:

- Sections 100.6 – 100.11: Conceptual framework approach
- Sections 100.12 – 100.17: Threats and safeguards

PRINCIPLES VERSUS RULES

The AAT could have a taken a **rules-based approach** to ethics. This would have involved creating a large book of rules trying to cover every possible ethical scenario that could be faced, with an answer to every single ethical problem. Instead, its code of ethics is based on fundamental principles, which you should apply in all your work. Legislation setting out ethical requirements in the US, included as part of the Sarbanes-Oxley Act on corporate governance, is rules-based.

This **principles-based approach** to ethics encourages a case-by-case deliberation, judgement and responsibility that can be applied to the infinite variety of circumstances that arise in the modern business environment. Hopefully, this will encourage a more flexible approach to ethical problems, whilst at the same time promoting ethical awareness. This approach is advocated by the IESBA *Code of Ethics for Professional Accountants* on which the AAT bases its ethical code.

Consider the pros and cons of the principles- and rules-based approaches:

Rules-based approach – advantages

- Rules are clear-cut, leaving no room for misunderstanding.
- The correct course of action is likely to be obvious.
- Rules-based approaches are easier to enforce.

Rules-based approach – disadvantages

- You can wriggle out of your obligations by finding loopholes; it is often said that rules encourage avoidance.
- Promotes a "tick box" mentality, with concern for the letter of the rule, rather than its spirit.
- Must legislate for every circumstance, necessitating a large number of detailed requirements.
- New requirements must be developed as circumstances change.
- There is a risk of getting swamped by the details and missing the big picture.

Principles-based approach – advantages

- Sets more rigorous standards of behaviour as you must comply with the spirit, not just the letter, of the requirements. It is often said that principles encourage compliance.

- Helps you see the bigger picture rather than just individual rules.

- Flexible – can keep up with a rapidly changing business environment and be applied in differing circumstances across the world.

- Promotes the development of ethical judgement and decision-making skills.

- Helps create a culture of ethical awareness.

- Encourages you to take responsibility for your actions.

Principles-based approach – disadvantages

- It is not always easy to find the right answer or even to identify the right questions.

- There may be more than one correct course of action and conflicting interests and priorities must be carefully balanced.

COMPLIANCE WITH THE LAW

In the UK, law falls into two categories:

- **Criminal law** – offences relating to persons or property that affect the whole community. Criminal punishment for breach of criminal law (for money laundering or fraud, for example) is most likely to result in fines or imprisonment imposed by the state. Criminal cases are **prosecuted** in a criminal court.

- **Civil law** – wrongs relating to conflicts between individuals within the community. A lawsuit for breach of contract, for example, is a civil action and the remedies awarded are designed to place the injured party in the position they would be in were it not for the breach. The concept of punishment does not apply. Civil cases are **heard** in a civil court.

Accountants are affected by a range of laws which they should be aware of. Some of them are not necessarily obvious such as **health and safety legislation, environmental regulations** and **employment protection law**.

- Members who are employees have duties under health and safety legislation to take precautions against risk of injury and to report potential risks to management. Members who are self employed have duties to protect the health and safety of their employees.

- All employees have a general duty to behave in ways that contribute to, and maintain, a healthy and safe workplace. Reckless behaviour endangers both yourself and others: creating the risk of accidents, fire, security breach and so on.

- Environmental regulations are often industry specific. For example, businesses operating in agriculture, construction, energy generation and food and drink manufacturing are likely to be subject to targeted environmental legislation. Many businesses producing hazardous waste or air pollution will be affected by some environmental legislation, such as the Clean Air Act or Hazardous Waste regulations. Employees have a duty to ensure they comply with the environmental regulations relevant to their industry.

- Employment protection law concerns rules on whether an employer can dismiss employees without being liable for claims for wrongful and unfair dismissal. It also includes legislation on treating employees fairly, for example without discriminating against them due to their age, sex, religion or sexual orientation.

When deciding whether or not behaviour is ethical, compliance with the law is assumed as a starting point: "the law is a floor". Section 1.10 of the AAT Code states that:

1.10 "The code is based on the laws effective in the UK **which members are expected to comply with as a minimum requirement**. Members working or living overseas are expected to know and apply the laws of the overseas country, having taken local legal advice if necessary. Where this code refers to legal issues, it does not purport to give definitive legal advice or to cover every situation, nor does this code highlight every legal issue that members may need to consider. Members who encounter problems in relation to legal aspects are recommended to seek their own legal advice."

The key point to remember about the AAT's Code is that it is **not legally enforceable**. It provides a set of guidelines set by the profession and failing to meet them will **not** result in a member breaking the civil or criminal law. Any penalties are at the discretion of the AAT and subject to the member's conduct adversely reflecting on the reputation of the AAT.

The AAT's Code does have **limits** as members are also subject to legal or other regulations depending on the work they do. For example members who are involved in investment business or whose clients are involved in investment business must meet the Financial Services Authority's (FSA) rules on holding clients' money.

BPP
LEARNING MEDIA

THE ACCOUNTANCY PROFESSION

We set out the objectives of the accountancy profession at the start of this chapter.

In the UK, the accountancy profession is largely **self-regulatory**, with the professional accountancy bodies each responsible for setting and upholding the ethical standards of their members.

The bodies themselves are under the supervision of the Professional Oversight Board (POB) of the Financial Reporting Council (FRC). It should be noted, however, that the AAT itself is not supervised by the FRC or POB. We examine the role of the FRC and its constituent boards below.

The Financial Reporting Council (FRC)

The FRC is the unified, independent regulator for the accountancy and actuarial professions. It was established to promote ethical financial reporting and increased confidence in the accountancy profession, corporate reporting and governance in the UK, through:

- The setting of accounting standards which guide how companies' financial statements should be prepared (standards are set by the **Accounting Standards Board** (ASB)) and

- The review of financial statements that have already been published (by the **Financial Reporting Review Panel** (FRRP)).

It also has responsibility for the following regulatory functions:

- Issuing auditing standards – through the **Auditing Practices Board** (APB)

- Oversight of the accountancy profession – through the **Professional Oversight Board** (POB)

- Setting high quality actuarial standards – through the **Board for Actuarial Standards** (BAS)

- Investigation and discipline – through the **Accountancy and Actuarial Discipline Board** (AADB)

The structure of the FRC is shown in the diagram below:

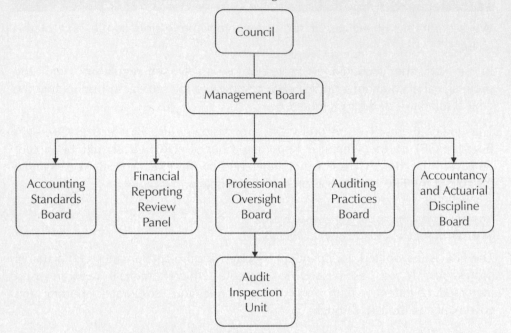

The role of the **Professional Oversight Board** is to provide:

(i) Independent oversight of the regulation of the auditing profession by the recognised supervisory and qualifying bodies
(ii) Monitoring of the quality of the auditing function in relation to economically significant entities
(iii) Independent oversight of the regulation of the accountancy profession by the professional accountancy bodies
(iv) Independent oversight of the regulation of the actuarial profession

The **Auditing Practices Board,** as its name suggests, acts mainly in relation to audit practices. In particular this involves establishing high standards in auditing, meeting the developing needs of users of financial information and ensuring public confidence in the audit process.

The **Audit Inspection Unit** carries out inspections and reviews of the audits of listed companies.

The **Accountancy and Actuarial Discipline Board** acts as a tribunal for disciplinary hearings, and can impose fines and other sanctions against accountants whose work fails to measure up to professional standards.

BPP
LEARNING MEDIA

Task 6

Which organisation of the FRC acts as an independent body responsible for monitoring the regulation of the accountancy profession by the professional accountancy bodies?

	✓
The Financial Reporting Review Panel	
The Accounting Standards Board	
The Professional Oversight Board	

There is a strong, growing international dimension to the regulation of the accountancy profession. The FRC oversees the profession in the UK, but while approaches differ across the world, national regulators increasingly share their ideas and practices, especially within the European Union.

There is also global convergence of accounting and auditing standards, which means that bodies such as the APB and ASB need to work with their counterparts from other countries. This work is carried out by international bodies such as the International Auditing and Assurance Standards Board (IAASB), which is part of IFAC, and the International Accounting Standards Board (IASB), which is part of the IFRS Foundation.

The International Federation of Accountants

Earlier in this chapter, we explained that the AAT Code is based on the *Code of Ethics for Professional Accountants*, produced by the IESBA which is part of IFAC. Let's look at the role of IFAC in a bit more detail now.

IFAC is an **international body** representing all the **major accountancy bodies** across the world. Its mission is to develop the high standards of professional accountants and enhance the quality of services they provide.

IFAC's mission is to:

- Serve the public interest
- Strengthen the worldwide accountancy profession
- Establish and promote adherence to high quality professional standards
- Promote further international convergence of these standards

To enable the development of high standards, IESBA, IFAC's ethics committee, established the **Code of Ethics for Professional Accountants**, which has aligned standards globally. All of the main accountancy bodies in the world are required to comply with its principles.

The code has the aim of identifying the responsibilities that a person employed as an accountant takes on, in return for a traditionally well paid career with high status. The code identifies potential situations where pitfalls may exist and offers advice on how to deal with them. By doing this the code indicates a minimum level of conduct that all accountants must adhere to.

The Consultative Committee of Accountancy Bodies (CCAB)

The major chartered accountancy professional bodies in the UK and Ireland joined together in 1974 to form the **Consultative Committee of Accountancy Bodies**. CCAB currently has five members:

- The Institute of Chartered Accountants in England and Wales (ICAEW)
- The Institute of Chartered Accountants of Scotland (ICAS)
- Chartered Accountants Ireland (CAI)
- The Association of Chartered Certified Accountants (ACCA)
- The Chartered Institute of Public Finance and Accountancy (CIPFA)

CCAB provides a forum in which matters affecting the profession can be discussed and co-ordinated, and enables the profession to speak with a unified voice.

The AAT itself is not part of the CCAB.

The AAT is a qualification and membership body for accounting staff. The qualifications of the AAT are vocational; members are accounting technicians who have practical accounting skills for use in the workplace. The qualification then allows a vocational progression route to the UK's chartered and certified accountancy qualifications.

It is worth noting that three of the bodies that make up the CCAB – ICAEW, ICAS, and CIPFA – are sponsoring bodies of the AAT. The fourth sponsoring body of the AAT is the Chartered Institute of Management Accountants (CIMA).

Financial Services Authority (FSA)

The Financial Services Authority (FSA) is an independent non-governmental body, given statutory powers by the Financial Services and Markets Act 2000. It is an independent body that regulates the financial services industry in the UK, including the running of investment businesses. It is accountable to Parliament via Treasury ministers. The statutory objectives of the FSA are:

- Market confidence
- Financial stability
- Consumer protection
- Reduction of financial crime

BPP
LEARNING MEDIA

The FSA regulates most financial services markets, exchanges and firms. It sets the standards that these organisations have to meet and can take action against them if they do not meet the required standards.

HM Revenue and Customs (HMRC)

HM Revenue and Customs (HMRC) is a government department that was set up in 2005, replacing the Inland Revenue and HM Customs and Excise. Its aim is to ensure that the correct tax is paid at the right time.

It collects and administers direct taxes (eg income tax, capital gains tax, corporation tax, inheritance tax and National Insurance) and indirect taxes (eg VAT, stamp duty and excise duties). It pays and administers child benefit, child trust fund and tax credits. It also protects us by enforcing and administering border and frontier protection, environmental taxes, national minimum wage enforcement and recovery of student loans.

Serious Organised Crime Agency (SOCA)

The Serious Organised Crime Agency (SOCA) is an executive non-departmental public body of the Home Office. Its aim is to tackle serious organised crime that affects the United Kingdom and its citizens. Serious organised crime includes Class A drugs, human trafficking, fraud and money laundering. SOCA is accountable to the Home Secretary and ultimately Parliament. This is set out in the Serious Organised Crime and Police Act 2005. In relation to this text, you need to know about the role of SOCA in money laundering, which we discuss in detail in later chapters.

Forms of regulation

Regulation is defined as the controlling of behaviour (individual or the organisation) by rules or restrictions. It can take many forms, including legal restrictions imposed by the government, and self-regulation by an industry (such as with the accountancy profession). Breach of regulations can result in sanctions such as fines, but note that this does not necessarily mean that a criminal offence has taken place.

Common forms of regulation include the following.

Self-regulation

Self-regulation is the process whereby an organisation or industry monitors its own adherence to legal, ethical, or safety standards, rather than have an independent agency such as a government entity monitor and enforce those standards. This is the model largely adopted by the accountancy profession in the UK.

Independent watchdogs

The term 'watchdog' is an informal name usually given to consumer protection organisations or campaigners. These bodies are set up to monitor and campaign for standards in particular industries.

Ombudsman

An ombudsman is a person who acts as an intermediary between an organisation and external interests such as the general public. You may have heard of the Financial Ombudsman who helps settle disputes between consumers and their banks or other providers of financial services.

Government regulation

This is regulation put into place by the government or government controlled organisations. Common examples of this form of regulation include controls on prices, wages, pollution effects, employment, standards of production and standards of service.

CODES OF CONDUCT AND CODES OF PRACTICE

When considering the control of ethical behaviour, codes of conduct and codes of practice are often mentioned. We shall now consider the differences between the two.

Code of conduct (employee ethics)

A **code of conduct** is designed to influence the behaviour of employees: it sets out the procedures to be used in specific ethical situations – such as conflicts of interest or the acceptance of gifts, and the procedures to determine whether a violation occurred and what remedies should be imposed. The effectiveness of such codes depends on the extent to which management supports them. Violations of a code of conduct may make the violator subject to the organisation's sanctions, which could even result in the termination of employment.

Code of practice (professional ethics)

A **code of practice** is adopted by a profession or organisation to regulate its members, and provide clear guidance on what behaviour is considered ethical in the circumstances. In a membership context, failure to comply with a code of practice can result in expulsion from the professional organisation. The AAT's Code of Professional Ethics is an example of a code of practice.

BPP
LEARNING MEDIA

Codes of conduct and practice often have a special legal status. They are **not legally binding** on employees and members – only legislation can do that. But if a company is being prosecuted, for example for breaking health and safety law, and it can be shown that its organisation's code of practice was not followed, then the court is more likely to find the company at fault.

Put more simply, codes of practice are used in support of legal duties and offer practical examples of good practice. They are not pieces of law in themselves but give advice on how to comply with the law.

BUSINESS ETHICS AND PROFESSIONAL VALUES

The concept of **business ethics** suggests that businesses are morally responsible for their actions, and should be held accountable for the effects of their actions on people and society. This is true for individual businesses and for 'business' in general, which has a duty to behave responsibly in the interests of the society of which it is a part.

In 'Setting the tone: ethical business leadership' by Philippa Foster Back (2005, published by the Institute of Business Ethics) the author lists some key business values such as truth, transparency, fairness, responsibility and trust.

The importance of business values in a company's culture is that they underpin both policy and behaviour throughout the company, from top to bottom.

Managers usually have a duty to aim for profit. At the same time, modern ethical standards require them to protect the rights of a range of groups inside and outside the organisation who have a legitimate interest or 'stake' in the organisation's activities. These groups are often known as **stakeholders**.

Business ethics are also relevant to **competitive behaviour**: there is a distinction between competing aggressively and competing unethically (for example, by stealing competitors' designs; using buyer power to prevent suppliers from dealing with competitors; or spreading false negative information about competitors).

A consequence of the need for a business to act ethically is for it to **change its culture** so all employees, managers and directors know what is expected of them. For example, management might 'turn a blind eye' to employees submitting inflated expense claims, but this is not something an ethical organisation would allow, so the attitude of employees and mangers must be changed so that only accurate expense claims are made

To achieve this a **code of conduct** must be developed and 'sold' to the organisation. The **Institute of Business Ethics** (IBE) was set up in 1986 to encourage high standards of business behaviour based on ethical values.

The IBE's website contains a lot of information on the purpose of ethics policies and programmes and also how to develop a code of ethics and make it work within an organisation.

The IBE also sets out the simple ethical tests for a business decision. Some companies provide their employees with ethical tests to help them make decisions, ie a series of questions to ask themselves. The IBE's simple ethical tests for a business decision are:

- **Transparency** ('Do I mind others knowing what I have decided?')
- **Effect** ('Who does my decision affect or hurt?')
- **Fairness** ('Would my decision be considered fair by those affected?')

Effective ethical programmes and codes of conduct

There are three elements to creating an effective ethical programme for a business:

Active leadership (setting the 'tone at the top')

The programme should be supported by the very top of the organisation. A senior board member should be appointed as 'Ethical Champion', whose initial role is to persuade all other senior executives to lead by example.

Buy-in

The Champion's next role is to organise a consultation process with members of staff to achieve their 'buy-in' to the new ethical culture. All staff should understand that the ethical code gives them principles and values that should be reflected in their everyday activities, and will help them deal with any ethical issues they come across while at work.

Training

Once employees understand the need for ethical behaviour and embrace the change in culture, training should be provided to ensure that all understand what is expected of them, and to further instil the ethical message. Helplines may be set up to provide employees with advice for dealing with ethical problems.

Benefits of a code of conduct

Organisations that develop and introduce codes of conduct find a number of benefits from doing so, which include:

Communication

Ethical codes communicate the standard of behaviour expected of employees and help them make the right choice between alternative courses of action.

Consistency of conduct

With the ethical message effectively communicated, the behaviour of employees can be standardised or made consistent across all operations and locations. Customers, suppliers and other stakeholders will receive similar treatment wherever they are.

Risk reduction

Standardised behaviour reduces the risk of unethical actions, as employees who are unethical will 'stand out' and can be dealt with. This reduces the risk of a few employees irrevocably damaging the reputation of the organisation and the trust people have in it.

Compliance with UK Corporate Governance

Corporate governance is concerned with rules and controls on how businesses are run. These rules and controls are usually put in place by the directors of a company. However, in recent years, non-legal guidance such as the UK Corporate Governance Code has been developed by the FRC that certain organisations (particularly those listed on the London Stock Exchange) should comply with or, if they do not comply, explain in their financial statements why they have not.

This guidance recommends that businesses draw up codes of conduct. The purpose is to ensure employees know what is expected of them.

The Nolan Principles of Public Life

The Committee on Standards in Public Life is an advisory body of the UK government which was established in response to concerns that conduct by some politicians was unethical.

A report by the **Nolan Committee** established **The Seven Principles of Public Life** which are relevant in part to accountants as there are some similarities with the fundamental principles set out in the AAT Code.

The seven principles are:

Integrity

Holders of public office should not place themselves under any financial or other obligation to outside individuals or organisations that might seek to influence them in the performance of their official duties.

Objectivity

In carrying out public business, including making public appointments, awarding contracts, or recommending individuals for rewards and benefits, holders of public office should make choices on merit.

Accountability

Holders of public office are accountable for their decisions and actions to the public and must submit themselves to whatever scrutiny is appropriate to their office.

Openness

Holders of public office should be as open as possible about all the decisions and actions that they take. They should give reasons for their decisions and restrict information only when the wider public interest clearly demands.

Honesty

Holders of public office have a duty to declare any private interests relating to their public duties and to take steps to resolve any conflicts arising in a way that protects the public interest.

Leadership

Holders of public office should promote and support these principles by leadership and example.

Selflessness

Holders of public office should act solely in terms of the public interest. They should not do so in order to gain financial or other material benefits for themselves, their family, or their friends.

Please note that leadership and selflessness are not really relevant to accountants; focus your attention on the other definitions.

Task 7

Which of the following is one of the Seven Principles of Public Life identified by the Nolan Committee?

	✓
Independence	
Openness	
Confidentiality	

BPP LEARNING MEDIA

RISKS FROM IMPROPER PRACTICE

There are a number of risks associated with doing business which mean that it is important for all employees, including accountants, to be vigilant. Maintaining an ethical stance in business dealings will help to ensure that a consistent approach is taken, and that as far as possible the effects of such risks can be minimised.

Operational risk

A particularly important risk is **operational risk**. This is defined by the **Basel Committee on Banking Supervision** (BCBS) as:

"The risk of loss resulting from inadequate or failed internal processes, people and systems or from external events."

An operational risk is therefore the risk of losses arising simply from the day-to-day business of the company – whether through its processes, its staff, its systems or from external events.

It is a broad concept including the risk of fraud, legal risks, physical and environmental risks. Risk management is usually carried out within the various business functions, and so it becomes an issue that affects every member of staff. For example, the IT department will take care of the risks associated with the processing, storage and use of information, and the human resources department will take care of personnel risks through its recruitment and selection procedures.

It is important to understand that the factors which contribute to operational risk (basically anything the organisation does in the conduct of its business) can be controlled to some extent by codes of conduct and an ethical programme. Therefore there is a link between good ethical safeguards and a reduction in operational risk and associated losses.

Types of operational risk

The following are the specific areas, listed by the Basel Committee, of operational risk for a business. Questions of ethics and ethical behaviour could arise in each one.

- Internal fraud
- External fraud
- Employment practices and workplace safety
- Clients, products and business practice
- Damage to physical assets
- Business disruption and systems failures
- Processes and delivery of outputs

Other types of operational risk include reputational risk and litigation risk.

Reputational risk is damage to an organisation through loss of its reputation. It can arise as a consequence of operational failures. So, for example, if a company performs poorly in answering calls at its customer service centre, because it does not employ enough staff, the reputation of the whole organisation could be tarnished.

Litigation risk is loss or damage which is the consequence of legal action or failure to follow a code of practice. For example, an organisation might have to pay damages to a customer for injuries caused to them by a faulty product.

Operational risk can be classified into:

- **Process risk** – losses resulting from poorly designed business processes

- **People risk** – losses resulting from human error or deliberate actions

- **Systems risk** – losses resulting from poorly designed systems such as internal and external controls

- **Legal risk** – losses resulting from failure to adhere to legal requirements

- **Event risk** – losses from one-off or on-going incidents such as a fire in a factory or the collapse of a market for the organisation's products

Types of event risk

One way of classifying event risks is according to their sources in the external environment:

- **Physical risks**: such as climate and geology, natural disaster

- **Social risks**: changes in tastes, attitudes and demography

- **Political risks**: changes determined by government, or by a change of government including changes in legislation and regulations, including the consequences of breaking the law or otherwise failing to meet legal duties or obligations

- **Economic risks**: changing economic conditions and operating environment including technological changes

Risk and accountants

All operational risks are real issues for accountants but there are safeguards in place to help reduce them. For example, following the customer due diligence rules required by the AAT's Code when new clients are taken on will help reduce operational risk related to business practice. These relate specifically to money laundering and we shall look at the details in a later chapter.

BPP
LEARNING MEDIA

Task 8

Damage to assets is an example of a loss resulting from which type of operational risk?

	✓
Reputational	
Litigation	
Physical	

AAT DISCIPLINARY REGULATIONS

We have considered above, the risks to an organisation of improper practice. There are also consequences for the individual accountant of non-compliance with codes of practice and regulations.

The AAT has a set of **Disciplinary Regulations**, available on its website, where it defines **misconduct** as a member having:

> "(a) conducted him/herself in such a manner as would in the opinion of the Investigations Team or the Disciplinary Tribunal, as applicable, prejudice his/her status as a member or reflect adversely on the reputation of the Association
>
> (b) acted in serious or repeated breach of the Articles or of any rules, Regulations or bylaws made under the Articles".

Who can make a complaint?

Paragraphs 7 to 10 of the regulations covering who can make a complaint and the possible grounds for action against a member are summarised below.

- Any person may make a complaint in writing to the Association concerning the conduct of a member.

- The Association shall consider and investigate any complaint provided it is made within six months from the time when it arose.

- Complaints made outside this time limit may be investigated at the discretion of the Chair of the Investigations Committee and the Conduct and Compliance Manager.

- The AAT can also commence proceedings if it becomes aware of matters concerning the conduct of a member which warrant inquiry.

BPP
LEARNING MEDIA

Grounds for Disciplinary Action

Grounds for disciplinary action exist if a member behaves in a way that prejudices their status as a member or reflects adversely on the reputation of the AAT. The Disciplinary Regulations identify the following events as conclusive proof of misconduct:

(i)   A member pleads guilty to or has been found guilty of an indictable criminal offence.

(ii)   A member becomes bankrupt or enters into any formal arrangement with their creditors.

(iii)   A member has not complied with Money Laundering Regulations

(iv)   A member has not complied with the AAT's CPD requirements.

(v)   A member unreasonably refuses to co-operate with an investigation into their conduct.

(vi)   A member in practice has failed to renew his/her practising licence before expiry.

(vii) A member has repeatedly failed to reply to AAT correspondence.

It is a duty of every member to inform the AAT of any event listed above that involves themselves. Failure to do this is also construed as misconduct.

The Disciplinary Process

Minor breaches of the AAT Code of Professional Ethics, which do not amount to misconduct, are dealt with under an '**informal procedure**' which involves contacting the member and informing them of the breach and advising them of any steps they should take to correct it.

Other complaints may also be resolved by **conciliation**.

The '**standard procedure**' is used for resolution of complaints not settled by the informal procedure or conciliation and consists of five stages, which are summarised below.

Stage 1   **Disciplinary investigation** to establish the facts

Stage 2   **Decision and recommendation** as to whether there are grounds for action

Stage 3   **Member's response** to those recommendations

Stage 4   **Preliminary matters and pre-hearing protocol**

Stage 5   **Disciplinary Tribunal** to hear submissions and witnesses

BPP
LEARNING MEDIA

The following disciplinary actions may be recommended for a full or fellow member who is found guilty of misconduct:

- Be expelled from the Association
- Have his/her membership of the Association suspended
- Have his/her practising licence withdrawn
- Be declared ineligible for a practising licence
- Have his/her fellow member status removed
- Be severely reprimanded
- Be reprimanded
- Be fined a sum not exceeding such maximum figure as the Council may set from time to time
- Give a written undertaking to refrain from continuing or repeating the misconduct in question

The following disciplinary actions may be recommended for an affiliate or student member who is found guilty of misconduct:

- Be declared unfit to become a full member
- Have his/her registration as a student withdrawn
- Be severely reprimanded
- Be reprimanded
- Be fined a sum not exceeding such maximum figure as the Council may set from time to time
- Be debarred from sitting the Association's assessments for such a period of time as shall be determined
- Have a relevant assessment result be declared null and void
- Give a written undertaking to refrain from continuing or repeating the misconduct in question

CONTINUING PROFESSIONAL DEVELOPMENT (CPD)

CPD was mentioned earlier in this chapter when we looked at the fundamental principle of professional competence and due care.

The AAT Code defines CPD as 'the process of a member continuously maintaining and developing knowledge, skills and competence to improve their performance at work'. CPD has a crucial role in ensuring that you maintain your **technical** and **professional competence**, and that you keep pace with changes in your work, including changes in the practices, techniques and standards of your profession.

The AAT has a regulation in force – Regulation 18 'Continuing professional development' – which sets out its requirements about CPD. There is also a CPD policy in place. These state that all members in practice must:

- Comply with the CPD policy.

- Comply with any directions given by AAT in respect of CPD.

- Keep adequate CPD records for the period of their registration or licence (ie a CPD plan, a record of learning activities undertaken and decisions made at each stage of the CPD cycle).

- Demonstrate compliance with the CPD policy when requested.

There are three routes to ensuring compliance with AAT's CPD policy. These are the:

- **Personal route**
- **Accredited employer route**
- **IFAC body recognition route**

The route we will describe here is that of the **personal route**. Members in practice must generally follow this route.

It is a condition of AAT membership that **all** AAT full and fellow members comply with AAT's CPD policy and complete a **four-step CPD cycle at least once in a 12 month period (twice for members in practice).**

This four-step cycle consists of:

- **Assessing** your learning and development needs for the year (or half-year) ahead

- **Planning** the learning activity you will undertake

- Putting the learning plan into **action**

- **Evaluating** the outcomes at the end of the year (or half-year)

BPP
LEARNING MEDIA

To demonstrate that they have complied with AAT's CPD policy members must keep adequate CPD records.

AAT monitors the CPD of members by conducting monitoring programmes twice a year. These involve checking CPD compliance of a sample of full and fellow AAT members selected both randomly and on the basis of risk.

It is up to those members selected to demonstrate that they have complied with the CPD requirements. If AAT concludes a member's CPD records do not confirm the member's compliance with AAT policy, it will provide guidance on how to do so in the future.

If a member does not comply with the CPD policy, they are helped to meet compliance, but in cases of persistent or wilful non-compliance or non-response to monitoring correspondence from the AAT, disciplinary proceedings will ensue. This could result in the member's expulsion from the AAT (although the AAT intends to help members with their CPD so this situation does not arise).

Under the accredited employer route, if a member works for an accredited employer, then they will meet AAT's CPD requirement by being employed by this organisation and following its learning and development processes.

Under the IFAC body recognition route, if a member holds full or fellow membership with an IFAC full member body (eg ACCA, CIPFA, CIMA, ICAEW or ICAS), they will automatically meet AAT's CPD policy if they also comply with that member body's CPD scheme. They may, however, still be selected for monitoring by AAT.

HOW IT WORKS

Some training needs will emerge in the course of your work. If your organisation introduces new equipment or software, you may need to learn how to use it! You may also identify your own shortcomings (missed deadlines, subjects on which you had to get help from others, times when you did not get the results you wanted) as learning opportunities.

Training needs may also be identified for you, as you get informal performance feedback from your supervisors and colleagues – or through formal appraisal interviews.

Other training needs may be identified as you keep in touch with developments in your professional environment: through the internet, professional journals (such as Accounting Technician), and networking opportunities through your professional body.

There is a huge menu of learning resources and opportunities available for you to use in order to meet you training needs, including:

- Courses, workshops and information seminars

- Books, quality newspapers, professional journals and technical publications (such as accounting standards, legislation and court reports)

- Videos, CD-ROM and computer software packages for education and training

- Web sites (for information and accessing training and materials)

- Instruction and procedure manuals used in your organisation (e.g. to teach you to use equipment and software, or to comply with organisational procedures and practices)

And there are two other very valuable sources of learning:

- **Other people**

   Your superiors and colleagues at work are an excellent potential source of information, advice and instruction/coaching in areas where they are more expert or experienced than you are. They may be able to help you access opportunities (eg nominating you for training programmes or secondments). They are also in an ideal position to offer you feedback (about your strengths and weaknesses, learning/improvement needs and how you are doing in your learning).

   Professional networks provide similar support and guidance within your wider professional sphere.

- **Your own experience**

   'Doing something' is an important development technique! Identify opportunities to try a new technique or approach at work, which you could use as a learning opportunity. If you want to learn to contribute more effectively to meetings, for example, what meetings could you arrange to participate in and observe? Whom could you ask for feedback?

➡ Signpost

See the AAT Code of Professional Ethics:

Section 1.14 Objectives of the accountancy profession

Section 100.5 Fundamental principles

Section 130.3 Professional competence and due care

Section 200.3 Self-employed members in business

See AAT Regulation 18 Continuing Professional Development

See the Appendix to Unit Guidance for PEAF: AAT Monitoring of compliance with CPD requirements

BPP
LEARNING MEDIA

Task 9

How often do AAT members in practice have to complete the AAT CPD cycle?

	✓
Annually	
Twice a year	

Task 10

If you ignore the AAT's rules on CPD you will be in breach of its Code of Professional Ethics and therefore liable for a fine under criminal law.

	✓
True	
False	

CHAPTER OVERVIEW

- **Ethical values** are assumptions and beliefs about what constitutes 'right' and 'wrong' behaviour. Individuals, families, national cultures and organisation cultures all develop ethical values and norms.

- **Ethical behaviour** is necessary to comply with law and regulation; to protect the public interest; to protect the reputation and standing of a professional body and its members; and to enable people to live and work together in society.

- The **AAT's Code of Professional Ethics** note that: 'the decisions you make in the everyday course of your professional lives can have real ethical implications'.

- **The five fundamental principles** described in the AAT Code are:

  – Integrity
  – Objectivity
  – Professional competence and due care
  – Confidentiality and
  – Professional behaviour

- The AAT's Code sets out a **basic problem solving procedure** for unethical action (the 'conceptual framework'):

  – Identify the threat to the fundamental principles that the action represents
  – Evaluate the threat
  – Apply safeguards to eliminate or reduce the threat
  – If safeguards cannot be applied, decline or discontinue the action

- The **principles-based approach** to ethics encourages case-by-case judgement.

- The accountancy profession is largely self-regulatory, with the professional accountancy bodies each responsible for setting and upholding the ethical standards of their members. This chapter looked at the roles of:

  – FRC
  – IFAC
  – CCAB
  – FSA
  – HMRC
  – SOCA

- A **code of conduct** is designed to influence the behaviour of employees; it sets out the procedures to be used in specific ethical situations.

BPP
LEARNING MEDIA

- A **code of practice** is adopted by a profession or organisation to regulate that profession.

- The IBE sets out simple ethical tests for a business decision:
  - Transparency
  - Effect
  - Fairness

- The concept of **business ethics** suggests that businesses and other corporate entities are morally responsible for their actions.

- Key issues in being an **ethical employee and colleague** include: not undertaking tasks that are beyond your personal experience and expertise; not undermining your professional colleagues; honesty; and ethical relationships.

- The **Basel Committee on Banking Supervision** has provided the following definition of operational risk; "The risk of loss resulting from inadequate or failed internal processes, people and systems or from external events".

- The AAT has issued its own **Disciplinary Regulations and defines misconduct as behaving;** "..in such a manner as would in the opinion of the Investigations Team or the Disciplinary Tribunal, as applicable, prejudice his/her status as a member or reflect adversely on the reputation of the Association".

- **Continuing professional development** activities ensure that you maintain your technical and professional competence, keeping pace with changes in your work role and the practices, techniques and standards of your profession.

- CPD involves both **formal and informal** learning experiences.

TEST YOUR LEARNING

Respond **to the following by selecting the appropriate option**.

Test 1

Only individuals can have 'ethical values'.

	✓
True	
False	

Test 2

The AAT needs to protect its reputation and standing by maintaining standards of conduct and service among its members in order to be able to:

	✓
Enhance the reputation and standing of its members	
Limit the number of members that it has	
Make sure that its members are able to earn large salaries	

Test 3

Which of these might (or might be thought to) affect the objectivity of providers of professional accounting services?

	✓
Failure to keep up to date on CPD	
A personal financial interest in the client's affairs	
Being negligent or reckless with the accuracy of the information provided to the client	

BPP
LEARNING MEDIA

Test 4

A client asks you a technical question about accounting standards which you are not sure you are able to answer correctly. 'You are supposed to be an accountant, aren't you?' says the client. 'I need an answer now.' What should you do first?

	✓
Say that you will get back to him when you have looked up the answer.	
Give him the contact details of a friend in your firm who knows all about accounting standards.	
Clarify the limits of your expertise with the client.	

Test 5

Put the four steps of the problem-solving methodology or 'conceptual framework' for ethical conduct into the correct order:

Apply safeguards to eliminate or reduce the threat to an acceptable level.	▼
Evaluate the seriousness of the threat.	▼
Discontinue the action or relationship giving rise to the threat.	▼
Identify a potential threat to a fundamental ethical principle.	▼

Picklist:

1,2,3,4

Test 6

Why are professional standards important?

	✓
It is in the public interest that employees who fail to comply with standards are prosecuted.	
It is in the public interest that services are carried out to professional standards.	

Test 7

Which of the following are member boards of the Financial Reporting Council?

	✓
Accounting Standards Board	
International Federation of Accountants	
Consultative Committee of Accountancy Bodies	
Financial Reporting Review Panel	
Professional Oversight Board	
Auditing Practices Board	
Financial Services Authority	
Accountancy and Actuarial Discipline Board	

Test 8

The Basel Committee on Banking Supervision defines operational risk as: "the risk of loss resulting from inadequate or failed internal processes, people and systems or from ..."

	✓
External events	
Government regulation	

Test 9

Which of the following are counted amongst the Nolan Principles on standards in public life?

	✓
Diplomacy	
Integrity	
Honesty	
Legality	
Accuracy	
Objectivity	
Accountability	
Openness	

Test 10

An AAT member who is found guilty of misconduct may be fined an unlimited amount.

	✓
True	
False	

BPP
LEARNING MEDIA

chapter 2:
BEHAVING IN AN ETHICAL MANNER I

chapter coverage 📖

AAT members may work for a commercial organisation in business or in practice with an accountancy firm. This means they perform a range of roles from processing invoices to preparing and reporting financial and other information, which their employer and third parties may rely on. They may also be responsible for financial management and advice on a range of business-related matters.

In this and the next chapter we shall build on the ethical principles which were introduced in Chapter 1 and identify how they should be applied in practice.

As you saw earlier, the AAT's Code has sections which are directly applicable to members in practice (part B) and members in business (part C). Where possible we shall consider the guidance applicable to each type of member together. Remember, you should be aware of all the rules, not just the ones applicable to your current role.

The topics we cover are:

- Acting with integrity, honesty, fairness and sensitivity
- Safeguards to protect against threats to fundamental principles
- Acquiring and working with clients

ACTING WITH INTEGRITY, HONESTY, FAIRNESS AND SENSITIVITY

You should have realised from Chapter 1 that accounting matters often require the use of personal judgement, and opinions as to the best or 'right' way to handle them can sincerely differ. Moreover, people need to develop their own ethical and technical judgement, as part of their own personal and continuing professional development. We shall now look at what behaving ethically means in practice beginning with acting with integrity, honesty, fairness and sensitivity in your dealings with clients, suppliers, colleagues and others.

Integrity

Accountants have a key role in preparing **financial statements**. Members in business may also prepare and report on a range of **information** for use by management and others – for example forecasts and budgets, costings, pricing calculations and management/business reports.

There is a clear need to apply the fundamental principles of integrity (not presenting untruthful or misleading information), confidentiality (not disclosing confidential information), professional competence and due care (preparing and presenting information in accordance with financial reporting and other applicable professional standards), professional behaviour (avoiding action that brings the profession into disrepute), and objectivity (presenting information free from bias or self-interest).

Part C of the AAT Code relates to members in business. **Members in business** are defined by the Code as members who are employed or engaged in executive or non-executive capacities in areas such as commerce, industry, service, the public sector, education, the not-for-profit sector, regulatory bodies or professional bodies, or members contracted by these entities.

As stated at the start of this section, members in business can be involved in the preparation and reporting of financial and management information that will be used by a variety of individuals, both internally and externally to the organisation they work for. The Code states that such information shall be prepared or presented '**fairly, honestly and in accordance with relevant professional standards** so that the information will be understood in its context' (s 320.1).

> ➡ **Signpost**
>
> See the AAT Code of Professional Ethics:
>
> - Section 320: Preparation and reporting of information

BPP LEARNING MEDIA

Honesty

Honesty simply means being truthful and not acting in a manner intended to mislead or deceive others. Using the work phone for personal calls when not permitted to do so and taking 'sick days' when you are not sick are fairly common behaviours – and your organisation's culture may have come to regard them as 'harmless' or even 'normal'. But they are still dishonest. Just because 'everyone does it' does not make it right.

Task 1

List some examples of behaviours that would be considered dishonest for you either as a student of the AAT or as an employee in a work context. Include an example of dishonest behaviour that the perpetrator might not even be aware was dishonest.

Fairness

Acting fairly means treating others equally. The increasing diversity of the modern workplace requires fairness, mutual respect and open communication, as the basis for constructive working relationships. As an accountant you not only have an ethical reason to be fair, but there is legislation in the UK which prohibits discrimination and harassment on a variety of grounds. These include race and colour, sex and sexual orientation, and religious belief.

Sensitivity

Sensitivity essentially means respecting another's right to confidentiality and privacy. Employers have specific duties to respect the confidentiality of employee information, but this should be extended to individual relationships – particularly if you have authority over others (and may be involved in counselling, disciplinary or grievance interviews).

SAFEGUARDS TO PROTECT AGAINST THREATS TO FUNDAMENTAL PRINCIPLES

We saw in Chapter 1 that the AAT's Code identifies five threats to its fundamental principles and some safeguards designed to protect against such threats. To recap, the threats identified are:

- Self-interest
- Self-review
- Familiarity
- Intimidation
- Advocacy

Since members who work in an accountancy practice are affected by different threats to those working in a commercial business, the Code makes specific recommendations to each situation.

The Code goes into considerable detail which is referred to below. However the potential threats and possible safeguards have been summarised in the following three tables, the first two of which describes some of the specific threats faced by members in practice and members in business respectively. The third table summarises the possible safeguards that can be applied in the work environment by both members in practice and members in business. We discussed the safeguards created by the profession, legislation or regulation in Chapter 1.

Threats: members in practice

Sections 200.5 – 200.17 set out examples of threats and safeguards that may be applicable to members in practice. The following table summarises the specific threats that may arise for members in practice.

Members in practice	
Threat category	**Specific threats**
Self-interest	<ul><li>Having a financial interest or joint financial interest in a client</li><li>Depending upon a client's fees for a significant portion of your income</li><li>Having a close personal relationship with a client</li><li>Having concerns about losing a client</li><li>Potential employment with a client</li><li>Contingent fees relating to assurance work (these are fees that depend on the results of the work)</li><li>Receiving a loan from an assurance client or from its directors or officers</li><li>Discovery of a significant error when re-evaluating the work of a member of staff</li></ul>
Self-review	<ul><li>Discovery of a significant error when re-evaluating your work</li><li>Reporting on the operation of systems after being involved in designing them</li><li>Preparing the data which is used to generate reports which you are required to check</li><li>Being, or having recently been, a director or officer of a client you are now auditing or being employed by the client in a position to exert significant influence over the subject matter of the engagement</li><li>Performing a service for the client that directly affects the subject matter of the engagement</li></ul>

 BPP LEARNING MEDIA

Members in practice	
Threat category	**Specific threats**
Familiarity	▪ Having a close or personal relationship with a director or officer of a client or with an employee of the client who is in a position to exert significant influence over the engagement
	▪ A former partner of a firm now employed in a senior position of the client so they are able to exert significant influence on the direction of the work
	▪ Accepting significant gifts or preferential treatment from a client
	▪ Long association of senior personnel with the client
Intimidation	▪ Threat of dismissal, replacement, or litigation in respect of an engagement
	▪ Pressure to reduce the quality of your work in order to keep fees down
	▪ Pressure to agree with the judgement of an employee of the client who has more expertise on a specific matter
	▪ Threat by an assurance client of not awarding planned non-assurance contract to the firm if it disagrees with accounting treatment for a particular transaction
Advocacy	▪ Promoting shares in a listed company which you audit
	▪ Acting on behalf of an audit client which is in litigation or in a dispute with a third party

Threats: members in business

Sections 300.7 – 300.15 set out examples of threats and safeguards that may be applicable to members in business. The following table summarises the specific threats that may be faced by members in business.

Members in business	
Threat category	**Specific threats**
Self-interest	■ Having a financial interest (eg shares or a loan) in the employer ■ Financial incentives and rewards based on results or profits (including commissions) ■ Opportunity to use corporate assets to your own advantage ■ Threats to your job security or promotion prospects ■ Commercial pressure from outside the organisation
Self-review	■ Being asked to review data or justify/evaluate business decisions that you have been involved in preparing/making
Familiarity	■ Having a close or personal relationship with someone who may benefit from your influence ■ Long association with a business contact, which may influence your decisions ■ Acceptance of a significant gift or preferential treatment, which might be thought to influence your decisions
Intimidation	■ Threat of dismissal or replacement over a disagreement over the application of an accounting principle or the manner in which financial information is reported ■ A dominant individual attempting to influence your decisions
Advocacy	There is unlikely to be a significant advocacy threat to employees of an organisation. This is because they are entitled and expected to promote the employer's position or viewpoint, as part of furthering its legitimate goals and objectives.

Safeguards

The following table summarises some key safeguards in the work environment available to both members in practice and members in business.

Members in practice	Members in business
▪ Development of a leadership culture in the firm that stresses the importance of compliance with the fundamental principles and acting in the public interest	▪ The employer's structures and systems for corporate governance
▪ Policies and procedures to implement and monitor quality control and require compliance with the fundamental principles	▪ The employer's own ethical codes and codes of conduct
▪ Policies that identify threats to the fundamental principles, evaluate their significance and identify safeguards to reduce or eliminate them	▪ Disciplinary processes
	▪ Strong internal controls
	▪ Quality/performance monitoring systems
	▪ Recruitment, selection, appraisal, promotion, training and reward systems that all highlight ethics and competence as key criteria
▪ Documented independence policies for firms that perform assurance engagements	▪ Leaders that communicate and model ethical behaviour and expectations
▪ Policies and procedures to identify interests and relationships between the firm or employees and clients	▪ Policies and procedures supporting employees in raising ethical concerns without fear of retribution ('whistle blowing')
▪ Policies to monitor fee dependence	▪ Forums for discussing ethical issues at work (eg an ethics committee)
▪ Using different partners and teams to provide assurance and non-assurance services	▪ The opportunity to consult with another professional (in confidence) if required
▪ Procedures that prevent non-team members influencing an engagement	
▪ Timely communication of all policies and procedures and providing education and training in all policies and procedures	
▪ Specified senior management in charge of quality control system	

BPP LEARNING MEDIA

Members in practice	Members in business
▪ Disciplinary procedures for failing to comply with policies and procedures	
▪ Published policies and procedures on whistle blowing	
▪ Engagement-specific safeguards (eg internal review, consulting a third party, discussing ethical issues with those charged with governance at the client, involving another firm to perform/reperform part of the engagement, rotating senior assurance team members)	
▪ Reliance on the client's safeguards (sole reliance on these is not possible)	

Task 2

An AAT member who works as part of an audit team having recently been a director or officer of the company they are auditing is likely to create which of the following threats?

	✓
Self-review	
Intimidation	
Advocacy	

➡ Signpost

See the AAT Code of Professional Ethics:

▪ Section 200: Threats and safeguards (200.5 – 200.17)

▪ Section 300: Threats and safeguards (300.7 – 300.15)

ACQUIRING AND WORKING WITH CLIENTS

Acting with integrity, honesty and fairness does not just apply to the performance of your work as a member in business or in practice. There are a number of principles which relate to the acquisition of clients that members in practice must apply.

Professional appointment

For all sorts of reasons, a client may wish to change from one professional adviser to another. They may be relocating, or looking for more (or different) specialised expertise – or lower fees.

The key point to bear in mind when accepting a new appointment is to ensure that doing so does not breach any of the fundamental principles – in particular AAT members must not accept work which they are not competent to perform.

Clients have the right to change advisers. The ethical issue is how to protect the interests of all parties, by ensuring that information relevant to the change of appointment is properly exchanged.

Guidance on professional appointment is provided in section 210 of the AAT Code (ss. 210.1 to 210.17).

The AAT Code states that **before accepting a new client**, members in practice must consider whether there would be any threats to the fundamental principles arising from accepting that client. Any significant threats identified must be mitigated with appropriate safeguards so that they are reduced to an acceptable level. What these principles effectively mean is that before accepting a new client, you should take into account any ethical problems that may arise as a consequence of it. For example, will you have the resources (staff, time, technical expertise) to give the client a quality service? Are there potential **threats to objectivity** (eg if you are related to an officer of the client company) or **confidentiality** (eg the client is a competitor of another client, and might pressure you to disclose information)?

Money laundering prevention procedures

The Code goes on to discuss the very important point of identifying and mitigating the threat of services being used to facilitate **money laundering or terrorist financing** (ss. 210.3 and 210.4).

The applicable anti-money laundering legislation in the UK consists of:

- **The Proceeds of Crime Act 2002** (as amended)
- **The Terrorism Act 2000** (as amended)
- **The Money Laundering Regulations 2007**

BPP
LEARNING MEDIA

The AAT has also provided its own guidance on compliance with **obligations** under the Money Laundering Regulations 2007. These obligations include customer due diligence on clients, reporting money laundering or terrorist financing, and record keeping. Failure to comply with these requirements results in a breach of professional behaviour.

We will look at **customer due diligence** now (since this must take place when accountants take on new clients), but we will look at money laundering in detail later in this Text, together with other aspects of compliance with money laundering legislation. Therefore it may be useful to return to this section again once you have covered the material in later chapters.

Customer due diligence provisions of the Money Laundering Regulations 2007 will apply in certain circumstances and when the relevant monetary threshold for a related occasional transaction (or series of transactions) is exceeded.

The regulations state that customer due diligence **must** be applied when:

- A member enters a professional relationship with a client which will have an element of duration

- The member acts in relation to a transaction or series of related transactions amounting to $\geq$ €15,000 (or the equivalent in sterling)

- There is a suspicion of money laundering or terrorist financing

- Where there are doubts about previously obtained customer identification; or

- At appropriate times to existing clients on a risk sensitive basis

Customer due diligence must be carried out on all **new** clients **before** providing any services to them.

The **one exception** to this rule is where undertaking customer due diligence would interrupt the normal conduct of business and the risk of money laundering and terrorist financing is very low. In this case, members must find out who the client claims to be before starting work and complete customer due diligence procedures as soon as reasonably possible afterwards.

For **new clients**, customer due diligence will start with finding out who the client claims to be and obtaining evidence to verify this.

Members also need to **obtain evidence about** individuals who exceed the ownership threshold and so are classified as **beneficial owners** of the new client. Beneficial owners are those **who own $\geq$ 25% of the client or the transaction property.**

Information must also be obtained about the **purpose and intended nature of the transaction**.

Evidence obtained may be documentary, data or information from a reliable independent source (or a combination of all of these forms of evidence).

A key point to note is that if customer due diligence cannot be completed (unless the exception described earlier is relevant), the accountant must not act for the client and must consider whether they need to make an internal report to their firm's Money Laundering Reporting Officer (MLRO) or an external report (Suspicious Activity Report, SAR) to the Serious Organised Crime Agency (SOCA), if they are a sole practitioner (these reports are covered in Chapter 4).

For **existing clients**, on-going monitoring must be undertaken. This involves carrying out appropriate customer due diligence procedures on any transactions that appear inconsistent with existing knowledge of the client, and keeping customer due diligence records up to date.

As stated earlier, customer due diligence must also be applied where there doubts arise over the validity of previously obtained customer identification information.

Transfer of clients

As well as acquiring new clients (and behaving ethically in respect of this), you may **receive a communication from a client**, saying that they want to transfer their business to another professional adviser. The AAT Code covers changes in a professional appointment in ss. 210.10 – 210.17. To behave ethically when ceasing to act for clients, the appropriate procedure is as follows:

Step 1   Respond promptly to all communications on the matter from your proposed successors.

Step 2   Disclose any issue or circumstance that might affect the successor's decision to accept the appointment – or confirm that there are no such issues.

One issue that may arise is if you suspect that the client is involved in money laundering: you *cannot* make any disclosures that might be used to 'tip off' a possible money launderer or terrorist (we shall look again at money laundering in more detail in Chapter 4).

Step 3   Once the change of appointment has been made, hand over books and papers promptly to your successor if asked to do so. However, there may be an issue if you have exercised a lien over them, in pursuit of outstanding fees (we discuss this later on as well).

Step 4   If your successor needs other information from you, in the client's interests, give it promptly (and without charge – unless it involves a significant amount of work).

BPP
LEARNING MEDIA

Recommendations and referrals

What about **recommendations and referrals**?

The AAT Code covers commission (including referral fees) in ss. 240.5 – 240.10.

A satisfied client may introduce others to your practice, and that's fine. You might also offer a **commission**, fee or reward to your employees for bringing in a new client. But you should never offer financial incentives to a third party to introduce clients (a referral fee or commission) – unless:

- The client is aware that the third party has been paid for the referral; and

- The third party is also bound by professional (or comparable) ethical standards, and can be trusted to carry out the introduction with integrity.

In the UK, if you receive a commission for introducing a client to another firm, and you are the client's agent or professional adviser you are legally bound to hand the money over to the client – unless they specifically approve your keeping it. Accepting such fees can give rise to self-interest threats to objectivity and professional competence and due care.

Members in practice might also pay a referral fee to obtain a client. This could arise in the situation where the client continues as a client of another firm but requires specialist services not offered by that firm. The Code states that such fees should not be paid unless there are safeguards in place to eliminate or reduce the self-interest threat to an acceptable level. In the case of payment of a referral fee, an appropriate safeguard may be to disclose this fact to the client.

Task 3

According to the AAT's Code of Professional Ethics, before accepting any new client relationship, a member in practice must consider:

	✓
How profitable the relationship will be	
Whether acceptance would create any threats to compliance with the fundamental principles	
Whether the client's directors meet the firm's moral and ethical standards	

Constraints on the services you can supply

Another point worth noting is that, for various reasons, you may not want to take on every client that approaches or is introduced to you! For example they may not offer sufficient profit or the work may be too specialised for your firm.

Additionally, the AAT's Code includes some constraints on the services members can supply; this is to protect against a member breaching the principle of professional competence and due care.

It is also worth noting that as an accounting technician, there are certain services that you cannot legally offer unless you are authorised to do so by the relevant regulatory body in the UK. These include: **external audit** of UK limited companies, or where the services of a registered auditor are required; **investment business** (including agency for a building society) and the provision of corporate financial advice; and **insolvency practice**. These areas (audit, investment business and insolvency) are known as '**reserved areas**'.

In addition, while you are providing public accountancy services, you should not at the same time engage in any other business, occupation or activity that:

- May threaten your **integrity**, **objectivity** or **independence**, or the reputation of the profession
- May prevent you from conducting your practice according to the technical and **ethical standards** of the profession

When considering accepting a particular engagement, you must also bear in mind any threat to the principle of **professional competence and due care**. You should only agree to provide services that you are competent to perform – or for which you can obtain the help, training or supervision you require in order to be able to perform competently.

Safeguards may include:

- Making sure that you have an adequate understanding of the client's business, and the specific requirements of the engagement
- Making sure that you have, or can obtain, relevant knowledge and experience, help or advice
- Consulting an expert, if required
- Making sure the timescales for the task are realistic (so you are not under undue time pressure)
- Assigning staff with the necessary skills
- Complying with appropriate quality control policies and procedures

BPP
LEARNING MEDIA

Conflicts of interest

We looked briefly at what conflicts of interest are in Chapter 1 and the AAT Code (Section 220) states a number of principles to deal with any conflicts as they arise. Conflicts of interest can result from a number of circumstances. Examples include when a firm undertakes services for clients whose interests are in conflict or where the clients are in dispute with each other.

The Code states that members must evaluate the significance of any threats. This includes considering whether the member has any business interests or relationships with the client or a third party that might give rise to threats. If any threats are identified which are **not clearly insignificant**, the Code suggests the following safeguards being applied (ss 220.3-4):

- Notifying the client of the firm's business interest representing a conflict of interest and obtaining their consent to act

- Notifying all known relevant parties that the member is acting for two or more parties in respect of a matter where their respective interests are in conflict, and obtaining their consent to act

- Notifying the client that the member does not act exclusively for any one client and obtaining their consent to act

- Using separate engagement teams

- Having procedures in place to prevent access to information

- Having a clear code for team members on security and confidentiality

- Using confidentiality agreements signed by employees and partners

- Regular reviews of the application of safeguards by a senior person not involved with those engagements.

The Code's guidance essentially means that when you accept a new appointment, or become aware of changes in the circumstances of an existing client, you should check whether this might create a conflict of interest with another client. The general principle is that the interests of one client must not have a negative effect on the interests of another.

An example would be if two client companies are in direct competition – and adverse disclosures or reports about one would benefit the other. Such conflicts create an ethical dilemma for the accountant, because it is impossible in such a case to act in the best interests of both clients at the same time – if you are required to make adverse disclosures about one of your clients, how is another, a competitor, to be expected to avoid making good use of them? It may also be an issue for a client, eg if they think there may be a risk that another client may (through the accountant) get hold of sensitive information.

If there is likely to be such a conflict of interest, you should:

- Put safeguards in place to avoid the negative effects, if possible (such as those described earlier as listed in the AAT Code).

- Avoid new appointments that might negatively affect existing clients.

- Disclose enough information to both parties, so that they can make a decision over whether to enter into (or continue) an engagement with you.

In large firms, this may be less of a problem, as completely separate teams can work on different client accounts. This is sometimes called 'building a **Chinese wall**' within the firm, between client affairs.

Task 4

The situation where a firm of accountants has two clients which compete with each other is likely to create a conflict of interest for the accountant.

	✓
True	
False	

Second opinions

In some instances, a client of another firm may seek your opinion on the advice they have received from that firm. This is known as a **second opinion**. There are a variety of ethical issues that this situation raises, such as your competence to do the work.

The AAT's Code covers second opinions in Section 230. The guidance basically states that members must evaluate the significance of any threats and apply appropriate safeguards if the threats are significant.

Appropriate safeguards could include:

- Seeking the client's permission to contact the existing accountant

- Describing the limitations surrounding any opinion in communications with the client

- Providing the existing accountant with a copy of the opinion

If the client does not give permission for the firm to contact the existing accountant, you need to consider whether it would still be appropriate to provide the opinion requested.

Fees and other types of remuneration

Accountants provide services for clients in return for fees which they usually charge on a **time basis**. This means the actual charges a client must pay are dependent on how much time the accountant takes to perform their work and how much they charge per hour. The ethical issues concerning fees are usually related to setting the hourly charge for different levels of staff and accurate time keeping.

Members can quote whatever fee they want to, but there are threats to the fundamental principles when fees quoted are so low that it is not possible to carry out the engagement with professional competence and due care. Safeguards include informing the client of the terms of the engagement including the basis on which fees are charged, and assigning appropriate time and qualified staff to the engagement.

As mentioned above, professional fees will normally be calculated on the basis of an agreed appropriate **rate per hour** or **per day** for the time of each person involved on the assignment. The 'appropriate rate' should take into account the skill, knowledge, experience, time and responsibility involved in the work. It also assumes that individuals give a 'fair hour's work for a fair hour's fees', in other words, that the work is efficiently planned and managed, so that clients get value for money. It may not be possible to state accurately in advance what the total charge for work will be. If there is any likelihood that the fee will end up being substantially higher than you estimate, do not give the client that estimate – or at least make it clear that the actual amount may be substantially higher.

It may, however, be necessary to charge a **pre-arranged fee** for the assignment, based on your estimate of how long the work will take; this is quite acceptable, as long as the fee is fair for the work – and the work is fulfilled on that basis.

Contingent fees

Contingent fees (or percentage fees) are those calculated on a predetermined basis relating to the outcome or result of a transaction or the result of the work performed.

This is customary for some types of non-assurance engagement where professional help is required to gain the client funds (eg selling an asset or recovering debts). If the assignment is not successful, the client may not be able to pay – and therefore, a percentage fee, contingent on results, is the only way they could gain access to professional services.

Be aware, however, that you *cannot* offer financial reporting services on a contingent fee basis - depending on a specific finding or result being obtained would present a major threat to your professional objectivity!

Again, safeguards need to be applied for any identified significant threats. These include:

- Advance written agreement on fees

- Disclosure to intended users of the work performed and basis of remuneration

- Quality control policies and procedures

- Review by an independent third party of the work done

Expenses

Out-of-pocket expenses that are directly related to the work performed for a particular client (such as travelling expenses) may be charged to the client, for reimbursement, in addition to professional fees.

HOW IT WORKS

You have just had a phone call from a prospective new client, asking about fees. You offer a free-of-charge consultation to discuss the matter. The client has recently left his job to become a freelance photographer; in the first instance, he requires an accountant to prepare financial statements and tax returns, and to advise on financial management.

'How much will you charge per year?' he asks. You explain that your fees are based on an hourly rate, which you quote to him.

'Yes, but how much in total?' he asks. You explain that it will depend on the work involved. You could make an estimate – but you would need authorisation from the partner to whom you report. Moreover, the client would have to be aware that the amount actually billed could be substantially higher, for example, if the client's business arrangements proved to be different from that anticipated.

'Do you reduce the fee if you don't save me as much tax as you thought?' the client asks. You explain that you cannot set a contingent fee on this basis, nor can you make any promises in relation to tax savings. 'What about if I get you to help me with a proposal for an Arts Grant that's available for photographers?' he persists. 'Will you accept a commission on that, instead of an hourly rate?' You agree that this would be possible.

'What about expenses?' pursues the client. 'Will I be paying for all this nice office space?' 'No', you explain. 'This is covered in our overall charge-out rates; you will only be charged out-of-pocket expenses directly related to my work for you.'

BPP
LEARNING MEDIA

Marketing professional services

To attract new clients, accountancy practices may **advertise** their services to the public and businesses. As in any form of advertising there are risks of misrepresenting your services and of making claims that damage the competition, either deliberately or negligently. In other words how a practice advertises itself, and how it tries to win an advantage over its competitors, is an ethical issue.

The AAT's Code covers marketing professional services in Section 250.

The guidance states that members must not bring the profession into **disrepute** when marketing their services. This includes being **honest and truthful** and not making **exaggerated claims** for the services offered, qualifications or experience, and not making **disparaging references or unsubstantiated comparisons** to the work of others.

The general principle is that a professional practice, and its individual members, need to:

- Project an image consistent with the 'dignity' (the high ethical and technical standards) of the profession.

- Maintain integrity in all promotional actions and statements.

Aggressive following up of contacts and leads is considered good marketing in some contexts – but it can be both counter-productive (by putting clients off) and unethical if you are promoting professional services. If you contact or approach potential clients directly and repeatedly, or otherwise in a 'pushy' manner, you may be open to a complaint of **harassment**.

Task 5

Advertising low fees to attract new clients is permitted by the AAT's *Code of Professional Ethics* providing they are justified by pointing out that competing firms are over-charging for their services.

	✓
True	
False	

➡ **Signpost**

See the AAT's Code of Professional Ethics:

- **Section 210**: Professional appointment
- **Section 220**: Conflicts of interest
- **Section 230**: Second opinions
- **Section 240**: Fees and other types of remuneration
- **Section 250**: Marketing professional services

BPP
LEARNING MEDIA

CHAPTER OVERVIEW

- Accounting matters often require the use of **personal judgement** – and opinions as to the best or 'right' way to handle them can sincerely differ. Moreover, people need to develop their own ethical and technical judgement, as part of their own personal and continuing professional development.

- Behaving ethically means acting with integrity, honesty, fairness and sensitivity in dealings with clients, suppliers, colleagues and others.

- Members in business and in practice face numerous **threats** against the AAT's five fundamental ethical principles. These threats can be classified as self-interest, self-review, familiarity, intimidation and advocacy.

- The AAT's *Code of Professional Ethics* provides one source of **safeguards** against the threats members face. Other sources of safeguards include the law, corporate governance rules and policies and procedures set out by their employer.

- There are a number of important principles and procedures to follow when a member in practice **acquires new clients**. At all times the law must be followed and respect and dignity should be shown to competitors and the accounting profession. In particular, rules cover:

  - Constraints on the services that can be provided
  - Dealing with conflicts of interest
  - Transferring clients
  - Money laundering regulations
  - Fees and receiving commission for recommending new clients
  - Giving second opinions
  - Marketing professional services

TEST YOUR LEARNING

Respond to the following by selecting the appropriate option.

Test 1

The fact that a client employs competent staff with experience and seniority to make managerial decisions can be used as a safeguard against threats to the fundamental principles by an accountant in practice.

	✓
True	
False	

Test 2

Accepting payment for introducing a client to another firm can give rise to which of the following threats to the fundamental ethical principles?

	✓
Self-interest	
Self-review	
Advocacy	
Familiarity	
Intimidation	

Test 3

Which of these represents a threat to professional competence and due care?

	✓
Providing a second opinion	
Accepting a gift from a supplier	

Test 4

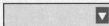 forms part of UK anti-money laundering legislation.

Picklist:

The Bribery Act
The Terrorism Act
AAT's Guidance on Anti-Money Laundering Legislation

chapter 3:
BEHAVING IN AN ETHICAL MANNER II

_____ **chapter coverage** 📖 _____

In this chapter, we continue our look at some of the specific situations that may be encountered in public practice or when providing accounting services.

The topics we shall cover are:

✍ Maintaining professional independence

✍ Acting with sufficient expertise

✍ Policies for handling clients' monies

✍ Confidentiality and disclosure

✍ Ownership and lien

MAINTAINING PROFESSIONAL INDEPENDENCE

An accountant has a professional duty to maintain an appropriate distance (independence) between their work and their personal life at all times. This is required in order to be able to act objectively, i.e. independence and objectivity are linked. We have already seen the need for independence when we looked specifically at conflicts of interest in Chapter 2 but the AAT's Code provides wider rules that you must follow in this regard.

Objectivity and independence are particularly important for AAT members who work in **practice providing assurance services,** such as carrying out a statutory external audit of their client's year-end financial statements which are then made publicly available and may be relied on by a number of users.

It is important to understand what an assurance engagement is, since this will help to explain why it is so important for AAT members providing these services to be independent.

An **assurance engagement** is defined in the AAT Code as 'an engagement in which a member in practice expresses a conclusion designed to enhance the degree of confidence of the intended users other than the responsible party about the outcome of the evaluation or measurement of a subject matter against criteria'.

This is quite a complicated definition with lots of terms in it, so to try and explain it we will look at an assurance engagement in terms of its elements.

An assurance engagement performed by an AAT member will consist of five elements:

(1) **A three party relationship.** The three parties are:

- The **member in practice** (or member of another IFAC body)

- A **responsible party** who is responsible for the subject matter (see below).

- The **intended user(s)**. In a statutory audit, the company's shareholders (who can be members of the public for large listed company) are intended users of the financial statements.

(2) **A subject matter**. This is the data to be evaluated that has been prepared by the responsible party. If the member is carrying out a statutory audit, the subject matter will be the client's financial statements and the directors will be responsible for these.

BPP
LEARNING MEDIA

(3) **Suitable criteria**. The subject matter is evaluated or measured against criteria in order to reach an opinion. In an audit, the auditor is judging whether the financial statements are true and fair, or are presented fairly in all material respects (free from material misstatements/errors).

(4) **Evidence**. Sufficient appropriate evidence needs to be gathered to support the required level of assurance.

(5) **An assurance report**. A report containing the member's opinion is issued to the intended user. For an audit, this is the auditor's report addressed to the shareholders.

You should be able to see that for the opinion given in an assurance engagement to be valued by the intended user, the AAT member must be independent, and in particular they should not be unduly influenced by the responsible party.

AAT members therefore need to **maintain independence from their assurance clients**, in order to protect the integrity of their professional services.

The AAT Code also considers **review engagements.** A review engagement is a form of assurance engagement which offers a lower level of assurance than an audit, since the procedures used in a review engagement would not provide all the evidence needed in an audit. Nevertheless, a review engagement is still an assurance engagement and the independence of the accountant is still important.

In a review engagement the AAT member in practice will conclude on whether or not anything has come to his or her attention that causes the member to believe the financial statements are **not** prepared in all material respects, in accordance with an applicable financial reporting framework.

Review and assurance engagements are covered in Section 290 of the AAT Code which addresses the independence requirements for such engagements in which a member in practice expresses a conclusion of financial statements. The Code points out that, for the reasons discussed earlier, members of review or assurance engagements should be independent of their clients and that this is in the public interest.

Section 290 also explains that independence requires both **independence of mind** and **independence in appearance** (defined below). These are necessary to enable the member to express a conclusion that is (and can be seen to be) free of bias, conflict of interest or undue influence of others.

- **Being independent**: the AAT Code refers to **independence of mind** as the state of mind that permits the expression of a conclusion without being affected by influences that compromise professional judgement, allowing an individual to act with integrity and exercise objectivity and professional scepticism (s. 290.4). This is the ability to put aside all considerations that are not relevant to the decision or task in hand, remaining free from bias, prejudice or partiality.

- **Being seen to be independent** (**independence in appearance**): the ability to **demonstrate** independence by avoiding facts and circumstances that would cause a reasonable and informed third party (who knows about any safeguards in place) to conclude that a member's integrity, objectivity or professional scepticism has been compromised (s. 290.4). Examples of circumstances to be avoided include clear **threats to objectivity** such as a personal financial interest in the outcome; a personal relationship with the client; or managerial/operational involvement in activities being reviewed.

Perhaps the most important way of maintaining independence is to be aware that you may be exposed to influences, pressures and other threats to your objectivity.

If you are aware of these pressures, you can analyse them and judge whether there are sufficient **safeguards** in place to reduce the risk of compromise to acceptable levels.

General safeguards include:

- Your own strength of character and professionalism, which enable you to stand up to pressure from a supervisor or client and do the right thing

- Your awareness of your legal accountability, and potential penalties under the law

- Your awareness of your professional accountability, and disciplinary action that may be taken against you by your professional body

- Your awareness of potential negative impact on your professional reputation (and future livelihood)

The AAT Code advises a conceptual approach to independence, and we discussed the conceptual approach to ethics in Chapter 1. There is more detailed guidance on the application of the conceptual approach to review and assurance engagements in the AAT *Code of Professional Ethics: Independence Requirements for Review and Assurance Engagements*.

Task 1

Avoiding situations that would cause a reasonable and informed observer to question your ability to be objective is known as:

	✓
Independence of mind	
Independence in appearance	
Being independent	

BPP LEARNING MEDIA

We shall now consider some more specific rules on objectivity and independence.

Objectivity and independence – members in practice

The fundamental principle of objectivity requires AAT members not to compromise their professional judgement due to bias, conflict of interest or undue influence of others. Above we talked about the importance of remaining independent when providing **assurance services**, such as when carrying out an audit of a company's year-end financial statements.

Objectivity and independence are often under the spotlight more with assurance services due to the reliance users of the financial information place on the resulting reports produced by the professional.

However, it is important to consider whether you are being objective, whatever the professional service offered.

As a result the AAT's Code provides advice on how members can maintain their objectivity in relation to **all services** in Section 280. It states that members in practice must consider whether there are any threats to objectivity specifically from having **interests in, or relationships with, a client or directors, officers or employees of a client**. One example given by the AAT Code is that a familiarity threat to objectivity may be created from a close personal or business relationship.

Where significant threats to objectivity are identified, safeguards have to be applied to eliminate or reduce the threats to an acceptable level. These could include the following:

- Withdrawing from the engagement team
- Supervisory procedures
- Terminating the financial/business relationship
- Discussions with senior management in the firm
- Discussions with those charged with governance at the client

If there are no safeguards that can eliminate or reduce the threat to an acceptable level, the engagement must be declined or terminated.

Before you decide to accept a new appointment or engagement (or to continue with an existing one), you need to consider:

- Potential **threats to objectivity** that may arise – or appear to arise – from the context and/or the people connected with the work

- What **safeguards** can be put in place to offset the threats – and whether these are sufficient to protect your objectivity (and hence independence)

There are specific situations or threats associated with a lack of professional distance between professional duties and personal life ie a lack of independence. These can be relevant to members in business and in practice. We have already considered one such threat – a conflict of interest – in Chapter 2. Now we look at others.

Financial interests (relevant to members in business)

There are a number of ways in which an accountant in business could gain financially from their activities for an employer – and many of these might pose a **self-interest threat** to fundamental ethical principles such as integrity, confidentiality, or objectivity. Other potential threats might be where the accountant, or someone close to the accountant, holds a financial interest (eg a loan or shares), is eligible for a profit-related bonus or holds, or is eligible for, share options in the employing organisation. The decisions and reports made or influenced by an accountant may affect the value of such interests (eg by inflating profit figures or enhancing share values).

The AAT Code defines a **financial interest** as 'an interest in an equity or other security, debenture, loan or other debt instrument of an entity, including rights and obligations to acquire such an interest and derivatives directly related to such interest'.

Financial interests can be direct or indirect. Again, the Code defines both of these.

A **direct financial interest** is 'a financial interest:

- Owned directly by and under the control of an individual or entity or

- Beneficially owned through a collective investment vehicle, estate, trust or

- Other intermediary over which the individual or entity has control'

An **indirect financial interest** is 'a financial interest beneficially owned through a collective investment vehicle, estate, trust or other intermediary over which the individual or entity has no control'.

The AAT's Code provides guidance to members in business on financial interests in Section 340.

The Code requires members in business to evaluate the nature of the financial interest, ie evaluating the significance of the financial interest and whether it is direct or indirect.

If significant threats are present (ie the interest is direct and of high value), safeguards will have to be put in place. If you think there may be an issue, you should consult with your supervisor, and perhaps with higher authorities. This might include, for example, an independent committee to set remuneration (for

senior managers) and the need to disclose relevant interests and share trading to the officials in charge of corporate governance in your organisation.

Other safeguards might include consulting those charged with governance or relevant professional bodies, internal and external audit procedures, and up-to-date training on ethical issues and the legislation relevant to potential insider dealing.

The bottom line is not to **manipulate** information, and not to **use** confidential information, for your own financial gain.

Gifts, hospitality and inducements

One of the key threats to independence and objectivity (and the appearance of independence and objectivity) is accepting gifts, services, favours or hospitality from parties who may have an interest in the outcome of your work:

- A work colleague (if working in business)

- A client (if working in practice)

- Any party with a current or proposed contractual relationship with your employing organisation: contractors and suppliers for example

These may be (or may be seen as) an attempt to influence the objectivity of your decisions, or to make you do or not do something. You do not personally have to be the intended recipient; gifts to your spouse or dependent children are assumed to be equally compromising.

Note also that if you offer gifts, favours or hospitality, this may be seen as an attempt to unethically influence others.

Does this mean that you cannot accept a bottle of wine at Christmas, or a calendar from a supplier? No. The gift needs to be significant enough that it could be reasonably perceived, by a third party who has all the facts, as likely to influence your judgement.

The AAT's Code sets out principles on gifts and hospitality to members in business and members in practice.

Rules for members in business

The rules on **inducements** under the AAT's Code are covered in Section 350. Inducements can include gifts, hospitality, preferential treatment and inappropriate appeals to friendship and loyalty.

Accepting significant inducements can give rise to self-interest and intimidation threats to objectivity and confidentiality. The question of whether an inducement is significant is one of professional judgement and to this end, the Code states that:

350.3 The existence and significance of such threats will depend on the nature, value and intent behind the offer. If a reasonable and informed third party, having knowledge of all relevant information, would consider the inducement insignificant and not intended to encourage unethical behaviour, then a member in business may conclude that the offer is made in the normal course of business and may generally conclude that there is no significant threat to compliance with the fundamental principles.

Possible safeguards to eliminate or reduce any significant threats to an acceptable level could include the following:

- Informing senior management of the firm or those charged with governance at the client

- Informing third parties such as a professional body

- Advising close or personal relations or associates of possible threats and safeguards

The Code draws the attention of members to the **Bribery Act 2010**, which we will consider later in this chapter.

Sometimes, members in business are expected to offer inducements to influence the judgement of others or a decision-making process or to get confidential information. The Code explicitly states that members in business must not offer inducements to **improperly influence** the professional judgement of a third party (s. 350.7).

Rules for members in practice

Similar guidance on gifts and hospitality applies to members in practice and is covered by Section 260 of the AAT's Code.

Accepting gifts and hospitality can give rise to self-interest and intimidation threats to objectivity. Again, the question of whether the gift or hospitality is significant depends on professional judgement and the Code provides the same advice on this as for members in business (s. 260.2 and s. 350.3).

Some appropriate safeguards to eliminate or reduce the threat to an acceptable level could include:

- Informing your boss if an offer (other than something clearly insignificant or customary) has been made

- Informing your boss if a close friend or personal relation of yours is employed by a competitor or potential supplier of your organisation (because an inappropriate appeal to your relationship, friendship or loyalty may be a form of 'inducement')

BPP
LEARNING MEDIA

The Code also directs the attention of members in practice to the Bribery Act 2010 which we will look at now.

The Bribery Act 2010

The Bribery Act 2010 is UK legislation which came into force in 2011. The legislation has been dubbed 'the toughest anti-corruption legislation in the world' and various concerns have been raised, particularly concerning its impact on UK companies that trade overseas.

The Bribery Act 2010 introduces four offences to UK law:

- Bribing another person
- Being bribed
- Bribing a foreign public official
- Failure by a commercial organisation to prevent bribery

Bribery occurs when a person offers, promises or gives a financial or other advantage to another individual in exchange for improperly performing a relevant function or activity.

The offence of **being bribed** is defined as requesting, accepting or agreeing to receive such an advantage, in exchange for improperly performing such a function or activity.

The Bribery Act 2010 does not explain what 'financial or other advantage' means but it could include contracts, non-monetary gifts or offers of employment. 'Relevant function or activity' is explained in the legislation as covering 'any function of a public nature; any activity connected with a business, trade or profession; any activity performed in the course of a person's employment; or any activity performed on or behalf of a body of persons whether corporate or unincorporated'. The Act explains that the activity is improperly performed when the expectation of good faith or impartiality has been breached, or when it has been performed in a way not expected of a person in a position of trust.

The Secretary of State for Justice, Kenneth Clarke, published guidance about the legislation three months before it came into force. This guidance identified six principles that all businesses should follow, which cover the following areas:

- Proportionate procedures
- Top-level commitment
- Risk assessment
- Due diligence
- Communication (including training)
- Monitoring and review

Companies will need to demonstrate that there are controls in place in each of these areas to mitigate the risk of bribery, should they or an employee be accused of bribery.

The penalties imposed if individuals or companies are found guilty of bribery are severe. Individuals may be imprisoned for up to ten years and face an unlimited fine. Companies may face an unlimited fine. In addition to this, there will be the associated bad publicity and loss of reputation.

Task 2

You have been recently employed as a payables ledger clerk for a construction company. Your manager has been granted ten tickets to attend the Ashes Test Match at Lords Cricket Ground, London, in a corporate hospitality box by a consultancy firm that is bidding for the contract to design your company's new computer system.

Describe the factors which will determine whether there is an ethical issue arising from the granting of the tickets.

Based on those factors, state whether you think the situation results in an ethical issue for:

- You
- Your manager
- Both you and your manager
- Neither you or your manager

➡ Signpost

See the AAT Code of Professional Ethics:

- **Section 280:** Objectivity – all services
- **Section 290:** Independence – review and assurance engagements
- **Section 340:** Financial interests
- **Section 350:** Inducements
- **Section 260:** Gifts and hospitality

HOW IT WORKS

At a training workshop, you are asking other accounts staff to discuss their ethical questions and concerns.

- One accounting technician feels it is dishonest to use work time and systems for personal emails. Another argues that this is part of the 'psychological contract': staff get paid slightly under market rate, so it's understood that small 'perks' can be taken advantage of, as long as the system is not abused. Lively discussion ensues as to where the line is between 'use' and 'abuse'.

- The first speaker accuses the other of dishonesty. You intervene and emphasise that no blame can be attached, since this has been a 'grey area' in the firm. Later, you take the accuser aside privately, and suggest that he gives some thought to the ethics of publicly criticising a professional colleague.

- One receivables ledger clerk compares your company's ethics favourably to those of his previous employer, and begins to detail its attempts to infringe copyright. You intervene, and remind him that he owes a duty of confidentiality to his former employer.

- There is some discussion about workplace humour. A cost accountant has been hurt by constant jokes about his religion. The others tell him to 'lighten up' but you draw the group's attention to the laws on religious harassment. The group grows thoughtful…

- Later, one of the staff approaches you and says that he has an ethical dilemma. He exaggerated his past work experience on his CV when applying for the job, and was not questioned on it in the interview. Now, however, he is being given tasks which he is not sure he is competent to perform correctly – but is afraid that if he says anything, he will be accused of getting the job under false pretences, and fired. You advise him to speak honestly with his supervisor – or at least to own up to being 'rusty' in this area: the important thing is not to take on tasks beyond his ability, and to get the help he needs.

We now look at this last issue, of acting with sufficient expertise, in more detail.

ACTING WITH SUFFICIENT EXPERTISE

We now look at the issue of acting with sufficient expertise. This is covered by the AAT Code in Section 330 and applies to members in business. The Code states:

> 330.1 The fundamental principle of professional competence and due care requires that a member in business shall only undertake significant tasks for which the member in business has, or can obtain, sufficient specific training or experience. However, if the member in business has adequate support, usually in the form of supervision from an individual who has the necessary training and experience, then it may be possible to undertake appropriate significant tasks. A member in business shall not intentionally mislead an employer as to the level of expertise or experience possessed and a member in business shall seek appropriate expert advice and assistance when required.

A member in business may be asked to undertake a wide range of tasks in the course of their work. Some of these tasks may be significant in their potential impact on the organisation and its stakeholders. Some of them may be tasks for which they have had little or no specific training or direct experience; tasks relating to a specialist field of accountancy, say, or to a specific industry sector or organisation type (such as charities) – or even unfamiliar software and systems.

Potential **threats** to the principle of competence and due care include: time pressure (when there may not be enough time to complete a task properly); insufficient or inaccurate information; lack of resources (eg equipment or help); or your own lack of experience, knowledge or training.

These threats may not be significant if you are working as part of a team, or under supervision, or on a comparatively low-level task. If they *are* significant, however, you may need to apply safeguards to eliminate them or reduce them to an acceptable level. These could include some of the following:

- Obtaining additional advice or training

- Ensuring you have enough time to do your work

- Getting help from someone with the relevant knowledge

- Consulting with superiors, independent experts or the relevant professional body

Much as you may enjoy a 'challenge', take great care:

- Not to mislead your employer by stating (or giving the impression) that you have more knowledge, expertise or experience than you actually have!

BPP
LEARNING MEDIA

- To state clearly and assertively that a particular task is outside the boundaries of your professional expertise and experience.

- To be realistic, responsible and proactive in requesting or accessing whatever extra time or resources, advice, help, supervision or training you need to deliver competent performance and to meet agreed deadlines. You may need help from outside the business eg from an independent expert or the relevant professional body.

If you cannot get the time, information, resources or help you need to do the job properly, you may have to refuse to do it – explaining your reasons clearly and carefully to your boss.

➡️ **Signpost**

See the AAT Code of Professional Ethics:

- **Section 330**: Acting with sufficient expertise

POLICIES FOR HANDLING CLIENT MONIES

AAT members who work in practice may come into contact with client monies. **Client monies** are any funds, or form of documents of title to money, or documents of title which can be converted into money that a member in practice holds on behalf of a client.

Client monies **do not include** fees for work done or fees paid in advance for work to be done, or the use and control of a client's own bank account. Although, if a member in practice has control over the client's own bank account specific written authority must have been obtained and acknowledged by the client's bank. This authority must have been obtained prior to the member exercising control over the account and adequate records of the transactions undertaken must be maintained.

Examples of client monies are;

- Refunds from HMRC received on behalf of a client

- Funds entrusted to a member in practice to assist in carrying out the client's instructions

- Surplus funds that fall at the end of an engagement

For example, the practice may be involved in paying a client's suppliers or employees. As a consequence it is important that a number of principles and procedures are followed to avoid threats to a number of fundamental principles.

Regulation 24 of the Regulations for Members in Practice sets out the rules AAT members in practice must follow when dealing with client monies.

These rules prohibit members from holding monies related to investments unless they are authorised to hold them under the *Financial Services and Markets Act 2000*.

Handling client monies is also covered in the AAT Code in Section 270. The Code states that members in practice must not take custody of their clients' money or other assets unless they are permitted to do so by law.

Handling clients' money – key safeguards and conditions

Holding client assets can result in self-interest threats to objectivity and professional behaviour. The AAT Code highlights some important safeguards related to **separation, use** and **accountability**

- **Separation** – clients' monies must be kept separately from monies belonging to the AAT member personally and/or to the practice.

- **Use** – clients' monies must be used only for the purpose for which they are intended.

- **Accountability** – members must be ready at all times to account for the monies (or any income, dividends or gains generated on them) to the client or authorised enquirers. (failure to do so can result in criminal and/or civil proceedings for theft and/or abuse of position)

The Code also states that members in practice holding client monies or assets should comply with the laws and regulations relevant to holding and accounting for such assets.

In addition to ensuring the safeguards above are in place, AAT members in practice must also ensure:

- Client monies are held in the same currency that they were received in unless the client has given instructions to exchange into another currency

- The client has been identified and verified on a risk-sensitive basis before holding monies on their behalf

When not to hold clients' monies

As a member in practice you should not hold clients' monies if:

- They are the monies of investment business clients and you are not regulated by the FSA.

- There is reason to believe that they are 'criminal property' (obtained from, or to be used for, criminal activities); this would constitute money laundering.

- There is no justification for holding the monies (eg they are not related to a service the member in practice provides).

- There is a condition on your licence or registration that prohibits you from dealing with client monies.

Fraud Act 2006

Another area to be aware of when considering the handling of client monies is the penalties for fraud in the event that funds are mishandled. Under the **Fraud Act 2006**, a person is guilty of fraud if they are in breach of any of the following sections of the Act:

- Section 2 (**fraud by false representation**)
- Section 3 (**fraud by failing to disclose information**)
- Section 4 (**fraud by abuse of position**)

It is Section 4 that is most likely to apply to a professional accountant holding client monies, who is tempted to commit fraud. A person is in breach of this section if they:

- Occupy a position in which they are expected to look after the financial interests of another person

- Dishonestly abuse that position and

- Intend, by means of the abuse of that position

   (i)   To make a gain for themselves or another, or
   (ii) To cause loss to another or to expose another to a risk of loss

Any person who is guilty of fraud is liable to a prison sentence or fine.

Task 3

Fill in the missing word below.

Section 4 of the Fraud Act 2006 covers fraud by [   ] of position.

HOW IT WORKS

Franklin Delaney, your new client, phones to ask if you would hold some money on his behalf, 'for reasons he would rather not discuss at the moment'. Although you have carried out due diligence in confirming Mr Delaney's identity and sources of income, you explain to him that you cannot hold any client monies without verifying the commercial purpose of the transaction and the source and destination of the funds.

Meanwhile, another client has deposited funds with you, pending completion on a house purchase; the client will be overseas at the time, and you have agreed to liaise with her solicitor to complete the transaction. It is agreed that your own fees may be drawn from the client account.

➡ Signpost

See the Appendix to Unit Guidance for PEAF: Managing client monies

See the AAT Code of Professional Ethics:

- **Section 270**: Custody of client assets

CONFIDENTIALITY AND DISCLOSURE

As an accountant, you are likely to have access to a great deal of information about the financial affairs of your clients (or your employers and their clients) that would not, in the normal course of business, be disclosed to the public.

All information you receive through your work as an accountant should be regarded as **confidential**: that is, given in trust (or confidence) that it will not be shared or disclosed. Confidentiality is one of the fundamental principles of ethics that we looked at in Chapter 1.

Examples include:

- Information shared with the explicit proviso that it be kept **private and confidential**

- Information shared within a **professional/client relationship** (eg with an accountant or solicitor), which is regarded as a relationship of 'trust and confidence' under the law

- Information that is **restricted or classified** within an organisation's information system (eg marked 'private', 'confidential' or 'for authorised individuals only')

- Information protected by **data protection and personal privacy law** (eg in the UK, personal data held by organisations, and personal medical data of employees, covered by the **Data Protection Act 1998**)

- Information that could be used **against the interests** of the organisation or an individual

The Data Protection Act 1998 and the Information Commissioner's Office

The Data Protection Act gives individuals the right to know what information is held about them. It provides a framework to ensure that personal information is handled properly.

Anyone (an individual or a company) who processes personal information (a 'data controller') must comply with eight principles, which make sure that personal information is:

- Fairly and lawfully processed
- Processed for limited purposes
- Adequate, relevant and not excessive
- Accurate and up to date
- Not kept for longer than is necessary
- Processed in line with your rights
- Secure
- Not transferred to other countries without adequate protection

The Act also provides individuals with important rights, including the right to find out what personal information is held about them on computer and most paper records.

Should an individual or organisation feel that they are being denied access to personal information, or that their information has not been handled appropriately, they can contact the Information Commissioner's Office (ICO). The ICO has legal powers to ensure that organisations comply with the requirements of the Data Protection Act.

The ICO maintains a public register of data controllers. Each register entry includes the name and address of the data controller and a general description of the processing of personal information that is being undertaken. Individuals can consult the register to find out what processing of personal information is being carried out by a particular data controller.

Notification is the process by which a data controller gives the ICO details about the processing of personal information. **Notification is a statutory requirement** and every organisation that processes personal information must notify the ICO unless they are exempt. **Failure to notify is a criminal offence**.

The notification period is one year, and data controllers must re-register. They must also keep the register up to date, so when any part of the entry becomes inaccurate or incomplete, the ICO must be informed within 28 days. Again failure to do so is a criminal offence.

The principal purpose of having notification and the public register is transparency and openness. It is a basic principle of data protection that the public should know (or should be able to find out) who is carrying out the processing of personal information as well as other details about the processing (such as for what reason it is being carried out).

Task 4

Fill in the missing number below.

The Information Commissioner's Office (ICO) maintains a public register of data controllers. If any part of a data controller's register becomes inaccurate then they should notify the ICO within ☐ days.

The duty of confidentiality

In Chapter 1 we studied the detailed requirements of the AAT's Code in respect of confidentiality, and we will not repeat them here, but you should remember that they state clearly that:

"...members have an obligation to respect the **confidentiality** of information about a client's or employer's affairs, or the affairs of clients of employers, acquired in the course of professional work."

This may seem obvious, but it extends more widely than you may think:

- It applies even after the assignment, or the contractual relationship with the client or employer is over. In other words, you need to respect the confidentiality of information about former clients and ex-employers too.

- It applies not just to you, but to any staff under your authority, and any people you ask for advice or assistance. It is up to you to ensure that they keep any information you share with them confidential.

BPP
LEARNING MEDIA

When *can* you disclose confidential information?

As we saw in Chapter 1, disclosure of confidential information is a difficult and complex area and members are therefore sometimes specifically advised to seek professional advice before disclosing it.

You are permitted to disclose confidential information in three specific sets of circumstances (see section 140.7 of the AAT Code):

(1) **When you are properly authorised to do so and this is permitted by law**

The client or employer may legitimately authorise you to disclose the information. However, you still need to consider the effect of disclosure; will it be in the best interests of all the parties involved in the matter?

(2) **When you have a professional duty or right to do so, which is in the public interest and is not prohibited by law**

You are entitled to disclose information if it is necessary to do so in order to perform your work properly, according to the technical standards and ethical requirements of the profession.

You also have a duty to disclose information if asked to do so by the AAT or another regulatory body, as part of an ethical or disciplinary investigation into your conduct (or the conduct of your employer or client).

Another example is to protect the member's professional interests in legal proceedings.

(3) **When you have a legal duty to do so**

UK law requires you to:

(a) Produce documents or give evidence if asked to do so by a court of law, in the course of **legal proceedings** against you, or your client or employer.

(b) Disclose certain information to bodies that have **statutory powers** to demand the information, such as **HMRC**.

(c) Disclose certain **illegal activities** to appropriate public authorities. Not all illegal activities must be reported in this way; there may be other regulatory machinery for dealing with them. However, some activities are covered by specific legal provisions, particularly in relation to public safety, organised crime, money laundering and terrorism.

HOW IT WORKS

Your in-tray this morning contains three requests for information:

- You receive a formal demand from HMRC for information regarding the VAT returns of a client.

  You report this to one of the partners, who says he will refer the matter to the firm's legal advisers.

- A property developer, who is a client of yours, has written asking whether you know of any businesses in the city looking to sell a commercial property.

  You recall that a petrol station client of yours has told you that they are intending to sell. However, you are also aware that the value of the property (for its current purposes) will fall once a scheme for a new by-pass is announced. Both these facts are covered by client confidentiality.

  You call the petrol station owners and ask them if you can disclose their plans to the property developer. They give permission, so you pass the message to the developer. At the same time, you advise him of the need to carry out 'due diligence' for any purchase, including checking any development applications already under consideration by the Town Planners – without suggesting any specific reason to do so. You follow up with a letter to both the petrol station owners and the property developers, recommending that they seek independent advice regarding the sale/purchase; this enables you to avoid taking on a conflict of interest between the two clients (if one wins and one loses from the transaction).

- A new employee has given you her banking details, for payroll. She has also included some information about the rates of pay and benefits paid by her previous employer, and some of its payroll practices – apparently just to explain how delighted she is by the generosity and integrity of your company.

  This data may have been given in good faith – but it is inappropriate to disclose confidential details of a previous employer. You delete the e-mail, having recorded the relevant banking details. You also make a note to have a quiet word with her about confidentiality.

BPP
LEARNING MEDIA

Factors to consider in disclosing information

Even if the information can legitimately be disclosed, you still have to consider a number of points in deciding whether or how to proceed:

- **How reliable is the information?** If all the relevant facts are known and supported by good evidence, the disclosure may be clear cut – but if all you have is unsupported facts, opinions or suspicions, you may have to use your professional judgement as to whether you disclose, how and to whom.

- **Who is the appropriate recipient of the information?** You need to be sure that the person to whom you give the information is the right person; in other words, they have a legitimate right to it, and the authority to act on it.

- **Will you incur legal liability by disclosing the information?** Some disclosures (such as reporting money laundering) are legally 'privileged' and you cannot be sued for breach of professional confidentiality. This is as long as the disclosure is made in good faith and with reasonable grounds. Other situations may not be so clear cut and you may need to consider getting advice from a solicitor before proceeding with a disclosure without the client's authorisation.

- **How can you protect the on-going confidentiality of the information as far as possible?** If you make a disclosure, you have a responsibility to ensure that it is made only to the relevant parties, and that they understand their responsibilities to protect the information from further disclosure. At least, ensure that you send the information direct to the relevant party, clearly labelled 'confidential' or 'for your eyes only'.

In Chapter 4, we will look at the specific case of disclosure of information by an employee of illegal or unethical practices by his or her employer – this is known as whistle blowing.

OWNERSHIP AND LIEN

Ownership of books and records

Accountants in practice base much of their work on the books and records provided by their clients and during the working process they generate working papers and files which document what was done. It is important to be aware of who owns the documents in the event of any dispute (for example regarding payment) that may occur. This is because very often the accountant will look to hold onto all the files until their bill has been paid by the client.

The ownership of books and records is mainly determined by **law** (check the position in your own country as we will refer to English laws as an example), but specific rights and responsibilities may also be as agreed in the **contract** (or letter of engagement) between the parties.

In general, if the accountant does not own the documents or records created, they are deemed to belong to the client, but the following factors must be considered:

- The **nature of the agreement** with the client (as set out in the letter of engagement)

- Whether the member is acting as **principal or agent**

- The **purpose** for which the documents and records exist

In common law, ownership depends on the **capacity** in which you act for the client:

- If you are acting as a **principal** (and not as an agent) for the client, documents and records prepared, acquired or created by you, for your own purposes, belong to you. Only documents that have been created by you on the specific instructions of the client belong to the client.

- If you are acting as an **agent** for the client, documents will generally belong to the client.

In accounting work, the **purpose** of the documents and records is also relevant:

- Accounting records and financial statements prepared for a client belong to the client. Your working papers belong to you.

- In taxation work, documents such as tax correspondence normally belong to the client.

- Written advice and supporting papers (on tax, investment or other matters) given to a client belong to the client – but your working papers belong to you.

- Letters that you receive from the client, copies of letters you send to the client, and your notes on discussions with the client all belong to you.

- Letters exchanged with third parties belong to you if you are acting as principal – and to the client if you are acting as his or her agent.

Lien

As we saw above, an accountant may seek to hold onto the client's documents until their fees have been paid.

In legal terms an accountant has a right (or **lien**) to hold onto documents that were used in performing the services until the fees are paid.

English law gives you the right to retain possession of the documents until your fees have been paid. (This is called a '**particular lien**' over the documents.)

You have a **right of lien** if the following conditions are met:

- The documents belong to the client (not a third party) *and*

- The documents have legitimately come into your possession and you have done work on the documents (eg have not been obtained under false pretences) *and*

- You have tendered an adequately detailed fee note – but the fees have not been paid in respect of *that particular work*.

The Appendix to the AAT Unit Guidance for Professional Ethics in Accounting and Finance contains detailed information on situations where a right of lien **cannot** be exercised, which you should refer to. The Appendix is reproduced in full at the front of this Study Text, but the following summarises the situations when a right of lien cannot be exercised:

- Statutory books and documents of a registered company which the company has to have available for public inspection

- Statutory books and documents of a registered company which the company has to keep at the registered office

- Register of members

- Directors' minute books

- Accounting records of a registered company (eg purchase invoices, cheque books, paying-in books, bank statements)

- Administrative records of a company that is subject to an administrative order, is in liquidation or has appointed a provisional liquidator (unless the documents give title to property, have been pledged or held as security for a liability)

- Records of a bankrupt person (subject to the same exception above)

It may be necessary to seek legal advice on the right of lien and to also consider other options for collecting unpaid fees. These could include the small claims court and the use of a debt collection agency. One thing to note is that an AAT member in practice in the UK who has obtained a court judgement for payment of a debt owed to him by a former client, must take action to enforce the judgement within twelve years.

Retention of documents

Accountants should keep hold of certain documents (such as taxation records and working papers) just in case they need to be referred to in future. For example, a client may be investigated by the tax authorities and your records are needed to show how their tax payments were calculated. However, there is the possibility that clients may attempt to sue the accountant because they believe they received negligent advice. In this instance the working papers may prove that the accountant acted properly.

The law on professional negligence requires that claims for negligence should be made within a reasonable time. Certain statutes specify the time periods within which actions must be commenced. Where statutes do not specify time limits, the **Limitation Act 1980** sets out the general position on time limits.

In the UK the time limit is six years for actions based on a simple contract or claim for civil damages. Six years is therefore the maximum time before which a disgruntled client could bring legal proceedings against the firm. Allowing another year to have it brought to court, **seven years** is probably the most sensible period to retain (and advise clients to retain) **books, working papers and other documents**.

Taxation records should be retained for **seven years** from the end of the related engagement.

There are also requirements to be followed on record keeping under the **Money Laundering Regulations 2007**. These state that records should be kept to assist in any future legal investigations and to show that the accountant has followed statutory requirements.

Customer due diligence identification evidence should be kept for **five years** from the date when the accountant's relationship with the client ends.

Customer due diligence information on transactions should be kept for **five years** from the date when the accountant completed the client's instructions.

HMRC has also issued guidance on its website on the record keeping for businesses and individuals. As a general rule, records should be kept for a minimum of **six years**, but there may be more specific rules for certain information. For example, PAYE records must be kept for three years; records for a personal tax return need to be kept for 22 months from the end of the tax year to which they relate.

BPP
LEARNING MEDIA

Task 5

Fill in the missing number below.

In the UK claims against an accountant in respect of a simple contract must be brought within ⬚ years.

➡️ **Signpost**

See the Appendix to Unit Guidance for PEAF: Books and records

CHAPTER OVERVIEW

- An accountant has a professional duty to maintain an **appropriate distance** (independence) between their work and their personal life at all times.

- There is a self-interest threat if members in business, or their close or personal relations or associates have **a financial interest** in their employing organisation.

- Gifts and hospitality (in the case of members in practice) or inducements (in the case of members in business) can also pose self-interest and intimidation threats to an accountant's objectivity and confidentiality.

- Potential threats to the principle of **competence and due care** include: time pressure (when there may not be enough time to complete a task properly); insufficient or inaccurate information; lack of resources (eg equipment or help); or your own lack of experience, knowledge or training.

- Key principles in handling or **holding clients' monies** are separation, dedicated use and accountability.

- Under the **Fraud Act 2006**, a person is guilty of fraud if he or she is in breach of its Sections 2–4.

- All information you receive through your work as an accountant should be regarded as **confidential**.

- The **Data Protection Act** gives individuals the right to know what information is held about them. It provides a framework to ensure that personal information is handled properly.

- **Data controllers** must register with the Information Commissioner's Office each year.

- You are permitted to disclose confidential information in three specific sets of circumstances: when you are properly **authorised** to do so; when you have a **professional** duty to do so; when you have a **legal** duty to do so.

- The ownership of **books and records** depends on legal provisions, contract terms, the capacity in which you act for the client and the purpose of documents and records.

- You may retain possession of documents (exercise a **right of lien**) in pursuit of unpaid fees in relation to those documents.

- Documents should be retained for at least the **period of limitation**, during which a legal action may be brought

BPP LEARNING MEDIA

TEST YOUR LEARNING

Respond to the following by selecting the appropriate option.

Test 1

Accepting gifts or hospitality from a client can give rise to which of the following threats to objectivity?

	✓
Self-interest	
Self-review	
Advocacy	

Test 2

Being bribed [▼] an offence under the Bribery Act 2010.

Picklist:

is
is not

Test 3

An AAT member in practice can keep client monies together with monies belonging to them personally, or the practice, as long as they have the client's permission.

	✓
True	
False	

Test 4

Notification to the ICO by data controllers about the processing of personal information is a statutory requirement, and failing to do so is a criminal offence.

	✓
True	
False	

Test 5

What is the most prudent period for books, working papers and other documents to be retained by an AAT member in practice?

 years

Test 6

You will always have a right of lien over client records if your fees have not been paid.

	✓
True	
False	

BPP
LEARNING MEDIA

chapter 4:
TAKING APPROPRIATE ACTION

chapter coverage 📖

Unfortunately, ethical issues are seldom clear-cut. You may often encounter situations where a course of action appears to be on the 'borderline' between ethical (or at least widely accepted) and unethical.

How do you know which is the 'right' course of action in a given situation or interaction? This chapter offers some guidance.

The topics we cover are:

✍ Identifying appropriate ethical behaviours

✍ Taxation services

✍ Money laundering

✍ Conflicting loyalties

✍ Dealing with ethical conflicts

✍ Dealing with illegal or unethical conduct by an employer

IDENTIFYING APPROPRIATE ETHICAL BEHAVIOURS

Ethics and the law

To be ethical, conduct must also be legal. You need to comply with the law, encourage your colleagues and employers (where relevant) to comply with the law – and advise your clients to comply with the law.

You may have encountered a range of legal issues in your personal life or workplace; be aware that these are all potentially relevant to professional ethics, insofar as they affect your behaviour and reputation as an accounting technician!

Task 1

Give five examples of laws that affect (or should affect) your everyday behaviour at work – not necessarily in the way you perform your accounting duties.

Critical decision-making on ethical issues

When considering what to do about an ethical issue, first of all, consider the application of available **legal** and **ethical guidelines** in the particular situation you are facing:

- How might the principles apply?
- Are there examples (or legal precedents) that might act as a template?

If the situation is still unclear, critical decision-making may be required. Two sets of ideas may be useful in helping you to reach a reasoned conclusion that will withstand later scrutiny:

- **Consider the consequences**. What will be the effects of the course of action – on you and others? An action may have both positive and negative impacts, or may affect some people positively and others negatively. However, a course of action that is likely to have an unacceptably high cost for any of the parties concerned may be said to be unethical.

  A basic test is to consider whether you would feel comfortable and confident, if you had to defend your decision or action before a court, or in the press, or to a moral/spiritual adviser you admire? If not, this may be an indication that, deep down, you know that it is potentially unethical.

BPP
LEARNING MEDIA

- **Consider your obligations**. What do you 'owe' other people in the situation? Some obligations are clearly set out in contracts (eg with employers and clients) – but we also, arguably, have a general 'duty' to treat others fairly and humanely.

   A basic test (using the 'golden rule', which is part of all major ethical systems) is to consider: would you want to be on the receiving end of whatever action you are about to take? If not, this may be an indication that it is potentially unethical.

So the key questions are:

(a)   Is it legal and in line with company policy and professional guidelines?

(b)   How will it make me feel about myself?

(c)   Is it balanced and fair to all concerned?

There are also outside sources of advice and guidance, which you may choose to access – but it is important to observe the requirement for **confidentiality** until you are sure that the situation is such that you have a right and duty to disclose it.

Getting help with ethical concerns and dilemmas

If you are employed by an organisation, any matter of ethical concern – whether or not it is explicitly addressed in the AAT's *Code of Professional Ethics* – should be raised with your immediate supervisor, if possible.

However, if the ethical issue concerns the organisation, or if you are self-employed, you may need to seek independent advice – within the requirements for professional confidentiality:

- Seek **independent legal advice** (particularly if there are potential legal consequences to your actions). Legal advisers are also bound by professional confidentiality, so this offers protection to you and the others involved in the situation. (Talking to a spouse, friend or colleague does not!)

- If you are still in doubt about the proper course of action, you can contact the **AAT's Ethics Advice line** (e-mail: ethics@aat.org.uk or telephone: 0845 863 0787 (UK) or +44(0)20 7397 3014 (outside UK)), presenting all the relevant facts.

Written records should be kept of any such discussions and meetings (as for other forms of conflict resolution at work), to ensure that there is evidence of the advice you have received. This will help protect you in any legal proceedings that may result.

HOW IT WORKS

At your firm of Chartered Accountants, you have been asked by the partner to whom you report to sit in and take notes as she interviews an applicant for the post of receptionist with the firm.

In the course of the interview, your attention is drawn to the following aspects of the discussion:

- The partner, having learned that the candidate has three small children, asks lots of questions about her plans to have more children and her childcare arrangements. When the candidate, in return, asks about the firm's family-friendly working policies, you notice that the partner omits to mention the childcare assistance that you know is available.

- The candidate reveals that the family depends mainly on income from her husband's job at a local electrical goods manufacturer. As it happens, this company is one of your clients – and you are aware of its plans to shut down the local plant over the coming year.

- The candidate left her previous employers because they continued to employ a successful member of their sales staff who had sexually harassed her and another female employee. This firm is another client of your firm.

After the candidate has left, the partner looks across at you and rolls her eyes and says, 'Just lose those notes, will you?'.

What are the ethical issues raised here, and how will you decide what (if anything) to do about them?

- The partner's focus on family responsibilities may be construed as sexual discrimination under UK law – unless she asks the same questions of any men she interviews for the job.

- Giving incomplete information about the organisation might be more significantly unethical if its effect was to mislead someone into taking employment under false pretences. In this case, not much harm is being done, as the candidate is merely being influenced against accepting a job that she probably will not be offered.

- You may feel sorry for the family, who are unaware that the husband will soon lose his job. But this is a fact of economic life – and you have the overriding duty not to disclose what you know about the client's plans.

- The behaviour of the candidate's previous employer is unethical. But you have come by the information indirectly – and is it anything to do with you? It would certainly be in your client's best interests not to risk legal claims against them.

- The partner's request to you to 'lose' the notes is ambiguous. It sounds unethical – whether as a suggestion of prejudice against the candidate, or as a way of dodging responsibility for the ethical issues raised.

So what might you do? First you might decide to clarify exactly what the partner meant; this would clear up any misunderstanding, and highlight the ethical issues more clearly. It might also be possible to draw her attention (respectfully) to the risks of her interview questions being construed as discrimination.

Other than this, it may not be your place to do much more – although you may choose to advise your clients of the ethical and legal considerations that have come to your attention: the need to be socially responsible in notifying employees as early as possible of impending redundancies; and the need for consistency, fairness and compliance with regard to disciplinary issues (such as sexual harassment).

TAXATION SERVICES

Much of the work firms of accountants do for individuals and companies concerns the preparation of tax returns and supplying tax advice. This can present the accountant with ethical dilemmas because clients want to minimise the amount of tax they pay, but the law requires the accountant to ensure they do not break the law.

The AAT Code provides guidance on taxation in Section 160. This states that members providing taxation services have a duty to put the **best interest of the client** forward, but this must be done **legally** and with regard to the fundamental principles of **integrity, objectivity and professional competence**. To this end, members must ensure that clients are aware of the **limitations** attached to taxation advice so that they do not misinterpret an expression of opinion as an assertion of fact.

Members must only perform taxation work on the basis of **full disclosure** by clients – it is the client who is responsible for the accuracy of facts, information and computations provided to the member.

Where members submit tax returns or tax computations for a client, they are acting as **agents** of the client. The respective responsibilities of the member and client must be clearly set out in the **letter of engagement**.

Where members in practice are acting for a tax client, they must provide **copies** of all computations to the client **before** submitting them to HMRC.

Members should take care not to associate themselves with a tax return or related communication if they have any reason to believe that it is **false** or **misleading** eg:

- If it contains a false or misleading statement

- If it leaves out or obscures information that should be submitted, in such a way as to mislead the tax authorities

- If it contains statements or information that have been provided carelessly, without the taxpayer checking or knowing whether they are true or false (and therefore being potentially false or misleading)

Tax errors and omissions are specifically mentioned in the unit guidance notes relating to the AAT Standards for this unit. If a member in practice or a member in business finds out about a **material error or omission** in a tax return from a prior year, or of **failure to file a tax return**, they must carry out the following:

- Advise the client or employer promptly about the error or omission.

- Recommend the client or employer to make disclosure to HMRC.

- If the client or employer does not correct the error, write to them to inform them that they cannot continue to act.

- Members in practice should report the client's refusal to the MLRO in the firm or to SOCA (if a sole practitioner), without disclosing this to anyone.

- Members in business should report the refusal and surrounding facts to the appropriate authority if that employed member has acted in relation to the error or omission. If they have not acted they are not obliged to report the matter, but making a report will not amount to a breach of confidentiality.

As well as the failure to report an error or omission you may come across another reason to report under the money laundering regulations if you are providing taxation services.

You should also note that for the purposes of the money laundering provisions, the proceeds of deliberate tax evasion – including under-declaring income and over-claiming expenses – are just as much 'criminal property' as money from drug trafficking, terrorist activity or theft. You therefore have a duty to report the client's or employer's activities to the relevant authority (such as the MLRO or SOCA in the UK).

Particular ethical issues are raised by performing taxation services (preparing tax returns, giving tax advice and so on), since there is a complex administrative and legal framework for both direct taxation (based on income, gains, profits and losses) and indirect taxation (such as VAT).

BPP
LEARNING MEDIA

The **AAT's sponsoring bodies** that deal with taxation (ICAEW, ICAS and CIPFA – see Chapter 1), and the **Chartered Institute of Taxation**, have extensive ethical guidelines in this area.

Key issues are **integrity**, **professional competence** and **confidentiality**. The general principles covered in the AAT Code apply to both direct and indirect taxation.

Task 2

What should you do if a client asks you how much tax you will be able to save them this year?

	✔
Provide them with a reasonable estimate based on what you achieved last year.	
Tell them that you will save them as much as possible.	
Tell them that you cannot provide such information.	

Task 3

What should you do if you become aware of a significant error in a tax return that you prepared and submitted for a client in a previous year?

	✔
Do nothing as admitting errors will damage your professional reputation.	
Correct the error by adjusting this year's tax return to compensate.	
Tell the client to advise HMRC about the error.	

A final thing to note relevant to ethical reporting in relation to taxation services is that **HM Revenue and Customs (HMRC)** has extensive legal powers to obtain information that may otherwise be withheld. If a statutory demand for information is made by HMRC, you should comply, possibly after seeking legal advice.

HOW IT WORKS

You are concerned about one your clients, a catering business. Although you are satisfied that personal expenditures of the owners have not been included in the financial statements of the business, you have not had an adequate response to a query you raised about undeclared income in its office catering arm.

The owners supply you with a general assurance, in writing, that all income is being declared. However, you have lingering doubts. The business is not reducing its purchases of supplies, nor the hours of its delivery staff – yet recorded sales are still very low when compared with comparable periods in previous years. At the same time, you note that mobile phone costs of all staff are being claimed as business expenses, on the grounds of 'extensive off-site trading'.

It is now time to prepare the client's tax return.

Having discussed the matter with one of the partners, you meet with the client to ensure that they understand that they are responsible for making full and accurate disclosure to the tax authorities, and are prepared to sign a statement to this effect. They reply that, as they see it, you are supposed to be 'on their side' to save them tax. You explain your professional and legal obligations and emphasise that you cannot knowingly associate yourself with a misleading return. As long as you have reason to believe that there may be errors or omissions, you will not be able to act for them in preparing or submitting this return.

> ➡ **Signpost**
>
> See the AAT Code of Professional Ethics:
>
> - **Section 160**: Taxation

MONEY LAUNDERING

A key example of the need to take appropriate action over illegal or unethical activities is the case of **money laundering**. We have mentioned money laundering already in this chapter when we discussed the provision of taxation services, as well as in earlier chapters in various contexts. In this section, we look at money laundering in more detail.

The AAT's Appendix to Unit Guidance for PEAF provides detailed information on money laundering and you should refer to it if you need to (it is reproduced in the front pages of this Text).

BPP LEARNING MEDIA

We have already mentioned the pieces of legislation that form part of the UK anti-money laundering legislation. To recap, these are:

- The Proceeds of Crime Act 2002 (POCA)

- The Terrorism Act 2000 (TA)

- The Money Laundering Regulations 2007

Money laundering is statutorily defined as an act which constitutes an offence under sections 327, 328 and 329 of the Proceeds of Crime Act. These are:

- Concealing, disguising, converting, transferring or removing criminal property (section 327)

- Taking part in an arrangement to facilitate the acquisition, use or control of criminal property (section 328)

- Acquiring, using or possessing criminal property (section 329)

Terrorism is defined as the use or threat of action designed to influence government, or to intimidate any section of the public, or to advance a political, religious or ideological cause where the action would involve violence, threats to health and safety, damage to property or disruption of electronic systems.

Importantly, there are **no *de minimis*** exceptions in relation to either money laundering or terrorist financing offences. This means there are no minimum limits to which offences relating to money laundering or terrorist financing can be applied. Thus, all offences which result in proceeds, however trivial, must be reported.

There can be no hard and fast rules on how to recognise it, but money laundering is generally defined as **the process by which the proceeds of crime, and the true ownership of those proceeds, are changed so that the proceeds appear to come from a legitimate source.** In UK law, it is an offence to obtain, conceal or invest funds or property, if you know or suspect that they are the proceeds of criminal conduct or terrorist funding ('criminal property').

The maximum period of imprisonment that can be imposed on a person found guilty of money laundering or terrorist financing is **14 years**. An **unlimited fine** may also be imposed.

You may think that you are unlikely to come across criminal property – but it is not all about the kinds of crime you see on TV cop shows! It includes the proceeds of tax evasion, benefits obtained through bribery and corruption, and benefits (eg saved costs) arising from a failure to comply with a regulatory requirement (eg cutting corners on health and safety provisions). Even small amounts are included in the definition.

Financial institutions and non-financial businesses and professions are required to adopt specific measures to help identify and prevent money laundering and terrorist financing, including:

- Implementing client checking, record-keeping and internal suspicion-reporting measures. This includes the appointment of a **Money Laundering Reporting Officer (MLRO)**.

- Not doing or disclosing anything that might prejudice an investigation into such activities. This specifically includes any word or action that might '**tip off**' the money launderers that they are, or may come, under investigation. You are, however, entitled to advise clients on issues regarding prevention of money laundering on a non-specific basis. We look at the penalties for tipping off later in the chapter.

- **Disclosing** any knowledge or suspicion of money laundering activity to the appropriate authorities. It is specifically stated that **accounting professionals** will not be in breach of their professional duty of confidence (and therefore cannot be sued) if they report, in good faith, any knowledge or suspicions in relation to money laundering, to the appropriate authority.

Proceeds of Crime Act 2002

The **Proceeds of Crime Act 2002** created a single set of money laundering offences applicable throughout the UK to the proceeds of all crimes. It also created a disclosure regime, which makes it an offence for an accountant as part of the regulated sector not to disclose knowledge or suspicion of money laundering. The definition of money laundering offences in the legislation includes even passive possession of criminal property as money laundering.

People who work in the regulated sector are those who provide specified professional services such as accountancy. This will therefore include AAT members in practice. 'Relevant persons' have a duty to establish and maintain practice, policies and procedures (ie customer due diligence, reporting and record keeping) to detect and deter money laundering and terrorist financing. Relevant persons are sole traders and firms (not employees) who operate within the regulated sector.

POCA established a number of money laundering offences including:

- Principal **money laundering** offences
- Offences of **failing to report** suspected money laundering
- Offences of **tipping off** about a money laundering disclosure, tipping off about a money laundering investigation and **prejudicing** money laundering investigations

BPP LEARNING MEDIA

Accountant's duty to report money laundering and terrorist financing

Under the Proceeds of Crime Act and Terrorism Act, accountants (including AAT members in practice) have a **duty to report** knowledge or suspicion about money laundering or terrorist financing when:

- The accountant knows or suspects that another person is engaged in money laundering or terrorist financing, whether or not he or she wishes to act for such a person or

- The accountant wishes to provide services in relation to property which he or she knows or suspects relates to money laundering or terrorist financing. If this is the case, the reporter must indicate in the report that consent is required to provide such services, and must refrain from doing so until consent is received.

If the accountant suspects another person is engaged in money laundering or terrorist financing, that person may be a client, a colleague or a third party.

There are, however, some **exceptions** to the duty to report.

The obligation to report does not apply if the basis of the knowledge or suspicion was not obtained in the accountant's normal course of business. For example a disclosure is not required if the information was obtained at a social event outside of work.

There is also no duty to report if the information was obtained in privileged circumstances (eg so the accountant could provide legal advice), or if there is a reasonable excuse for not reporting (as long as the report is made as soon as is reasonable in the circumstances).

If there is an obligation to make a report (a disclosure), the accountant must submit:

- An **Internal Report to a Money Laundering Reporting Officer (MLRO)**, if they are employed in a group practice.

- A **Suspicious Activity Report (SAR)** to the Serious Organised Crime Agency (SOCA), if they are a sole practitioner or an MLRO

A person commits an offence if he/she fails to disclose this knowledge or suspicion, or reasonable grounds for suspicion, as soon as practicable to a nominated officer (MLRO) if working in a firm, or SOCA, if working as a sole practitioner. The maximum penalty for failure to disclose is **five years** in prison or an **unlimited fine**.

The following information forms part of the required disclosure

- Identity of the suspect (if known)
- The information on which the knowledge or suspicion is based
- Whereabouts of the laundered property (if known)

Reports made under the Proceeds of Crime Act

A report made under the Proceeds of Crime Act is either:

- A protected disclosure
- An authorised disclosure

'Protected' disclosures are made by someone who knows or suspects another of money laundering and protect the person making the disclosure against allegations of breach of confidentiality.

An '**authorised**' disclosure is made by the money launderer themselves and should be made by a person who realises they may have or may be about to engage in money laundering, An authorised disclosure may provide a defence against charges of money laundering if it is made before the act is carried out or as soon as possible afterwards, provided there is a good reason for the delay. A good reason might be that at the time of the act the person didn't realise criminal property was involved.

Any person can make an authorised or protected disclosure. However, protected disclosures are compulsory in the regulated sector. Members in business should therefore make an authorised disclosure if they are personally involved in an act which might constitute money laundering, and they should encourage their employer to make a disclosure, but they are not required to as they are not in the regulated sector.

Tipping off

After a report has been submitted (even if the accountant did not submit the report but still knows about it or suspects a report has been made), the accountant must not subsequently disclose any information likely to prejudice any investigation.

If the accountant does make such a disclosure they are committing a criminal offence. The offence can apply even if it was not the accountant's intention to prejudice an investigation.

The maximum penalty for this tipping off offence for accountants is **5 years imprisonment or an unlimited fine**.

Prejudicing an investigation

There is also an offence that may be committed by **any person** (not just an accountant). This 'prejudicing an investigation' offence occurs when any person:

- Knows or suspects that a money laundering investigation is being (or is about to be) conducted; and
- Makes a disclosure which is likely to prejudice the investigation; or

- Falsifies, conceals or destroys documents relevant to the investigation, or causes that to happen.

As with tipping off, the 'prejudicing an investigation' offence can still apply if the person did not intend to prejudice an investigation when making the disclosure. However, there is a defence available if the person making the disclosure did not know or suspect the disclosure would be prejudicial, did not know or suspect the documents were relevant, or did not intend to conceal any facts from the person carrying out the investigation.

> ➡️ **Signpost**
>
> See the Appendix to Unit Guidance for PEAF: Money Laundering

HOW IT WORKS

When you visited your client's café business recently, you noticed that they had employed an additional chef – but now, checking the payroll reports, you cannot find any mention of this person, or any payments made to her.

You need to check that your suspicions (that the employee is being paid cash to avoid tax liabilities) are well-founded, but you are aware of the danger of '**tipping off**' the client.

This type of activity is known as payroll fraud. Payroll fraud is the unauthorised altering of payroll or benefit systems so an employee can gain funds which are not legitimately due to him/her. There are three main types of payroll fraud: setting up ghost employees, false wages claims, and false expenses claims.

Payroll fraud is an offence, reportable to the SOCA (or the MLRO in your firm); if you prepare financial statements covering it up, you are party to the concealment of 'criminal property'. Your first step is to discuss the matter with one of the partners. He advises you to speak to the client in general terms about the seriousness of accurate and truthful reporting. If the situation does not then change (and the payroll 'omission' is not put right), your firm's MLRO will be consulted.

Task 4

Fill in the missing number below.

The maximum penalty for being found guilty of money laundering is [   ] years in prison.

CONFLICTING LOYALTIES

If you are an employed member of a professional body, or a 'member in business', you owe a **duty of loyalty** to your employer and to your profession. The AAT Code states clearly that: 'A member in business has a responsibility to further the legitimate aims of their employing organisation. [Professional ethical codes] do not seek to hinder a member in business from fulfilling that responsibility, but consider circumstances in which conflicts may be created with the duty to comply with the fundamental principles'.

Where does your duty lie?

As an employee, your first duty will generally be to contribute to your organisation's objectives (ends), and to comply with all reasonable instructions, requests, rules and procedures (means) designed to further them. But what if some of these ends or means are unethical (as defined by the standards of your profession)? Where does your primary duty lie?

Your employer cannot legitimately require you to:

- Break the law

- Break the rules and standards of the accounting profession

- Put your name to, or otherwise be associated with, a statement which significantly misrepresents facts (particularly in connection with financial statements, tax or legal compliance)

- Lie to or mislead regulators or the firm's internal or external auditors

- Facilitate, or be part of, the handling of unethical or illegal earnings (i.e. money laundering)

The law and rules and standards of your profession take clear priority in such a conflict of loyalties: your duty is to refuse to obey the instruction or rule, unless it can be shown that it is not, after all, incompatible with legal and professional requirements.

This may be easier said than done, particularly if you are a junior employee and are being put under pressure by an influential (or personally overbearing) superior. You may need all your assertive communication techniques!

At the same time, it is worth remembering that not every difference of opinion on ethical issues is an ethical conflict – and not every ethical conflict is significant enough to present a real conflict of loyalties. In other words, pick your battles wisely!

BPP
LEARNING MEDIA

DEALING WITH ETHICAL CONFLICTS

The AAT Code sets out some advice to members in business concerning how ethical conflicts should be dealt with. It basically states that members in business have a duty to comply with the fundamental principles. However, there may be situations where their responsibilities to their employer conflicts with the fundamental principles. Where this happens, and compliance with the fundamental principles is under threat, members in business have to assess the threats and apply safeguard to eliminate them or reduce them to an acceptable level.

Safeguards could include:

- Obtaining advice from within their employing organisation, an independent adviser or a professional body

- Using a formal dispute resolution process within the employing organisation

- Seeking legal advice

What is an ethical conflict?

It is almost inevitable that at some time in your career, you will meet a situation that presents some kind of ethical dilemma or conflict, where:

- Two ethical **values or requirements** seem to be incompatible, eg you have the duty to disclose unethical conduct that has come to your attention – but also the duty of professional confidentiality.

- Two sets of **demands and obligations** seem to be incompatible ('conflicting loyalties'), eg if an employer or client asks you to break the ethical guidelines of your profession: falsifying a record; making a misleading statement; or supplying information 'recklessly', without being in a position to know whether or not it is true.

  Such situations may be particularly acute if you are put under pressure to do the wrong thing by an overbearing supervisor, or by a valued client, friend or relation.

Note that not everyone thinks alike on all ethical matters! It is quite possible that a fellow professional, or a work colleague, will honestly disagree with you about what constitutes an ethical or unethical course of action; this does not necessarily mean that you have an 'ethical conflict', or that you have to report and formally resolve the matter!

The kind of genuine ethical conflict that must be resolved is one that puts you in a position where you are being asked or required to take – or be party to – action that you feel may be unethical.

Resolving ethical conflicts

The AAT Code provides a structure for resolving ethical conflicts in Section 100.18 to 100.23.

If you are asked, instructed or encouraged to take a course of action that is illegal, or unethical by the standards of your profession, you are entitled and required to refuse.

This can lead to interpersonal – and perhaps even legal – conflict.

Some issues may be 'cleared up' by **informal discussion**; they may be based on a misunderstanding, or ignorance – or the belief that no-one knows what is going on! Your first aim will be to persuade the relevant parties not to take (or persist in) the unethical course of action.

If informal discussion does not work, and the issue is significant, more **formal** avenues may be pursued.

Whether informal or formal routes are taken, the member must consider the following factors:

- Relevant facts
- Ethical issues involved
- Fundamental principles
- Established internal procedures
- Alternative courses of action

Within an organisation (for members in business), there may be **established procedures** for resolving ethical issues and conflicts with colleagues or superiors, such as those for dealing with grievances. If this does not produce a satisfactory result, the problem should be discussed with the next level up in the management hierarchy, and/or arbitrators such as an Ethics Committee or those in charge of corporate governance (eg the board of directors or audit committee). If a conflict still exists after all internal avenues to resolution have been explored, the accountant may have no alternative but to resign.

Similarly, in a self-employed situation (for members in practice), if a client requests or instructs you to take a course of action that is unethical or illegal, you are entitled and required to refuse. The request may be made in ignorance and good faith – and you should attempt to explain the technical, legal and ethical principles that apply. If the client continues to insist, or refuses to change his or her own unethical conduct (where this reflects on you as his or her agent or adviser), you should simply cease to act for that client.

If the issue is unresolved, even if you have taken steps to protect your own integrity and reputation by resigning or ceasing to act, you may still have a duty to report illegal or unethical conduct to relevant authorities. This is a tricky area, because of the competing duty of confidentiality.

BPP
LEARNING MEDIA

HOW IT WORKS

You have some concerns regarding inaccuracies in the amounts of time some of your colleagues charge their clients which often result in clients paying for an accountant's time which has not been spent on the client's work. When you report this to the partner she says 'Forget it, the clients are still getting good value for money one way or another. Do you think the partners waste time tying down every hour that goes astray here or there? You worry too much.'

There will be an ethical conflict if you choose to pursue the matter (as compromising your professional ethics) and the partner insists that you let the matter drop. The culture of your firm, from the top down, is clearly unsympathetic to what are seen as 'minor' ethical concerns. You may have to go to the Ethics Committee (which should include impartial members), or get independent advice (from the AAT or a legal adviser) as to whether or how to take the matter further.

Meanwhile, you have sat in on another interview for the post of receptionist. This candidate, who is very keen and is currently working for another firm of chartered accountants in the city, appears to be the perfect person for the job. As the partner is bringing the interview to a close, the candidate says: 'By the way, I thought you might like to see the kind of systems I've got experience with. Here's a copy, on disk, of our Contacts Management software.'

After the interview, you tell the partner that you are not comfortable about this. She says that although it is, technically, a breach of copyright, she will destroy the disk after looking over it; this is probably within the definition of 'fair dealing'.

You suspect, however, that the candidate has actually handed her a competing firm's (highly confidential) client/contact list. This would clearly be unethical to accept, let alone use. Does the partner have similar suspicions, or is she acting in ignorance? Did the candidate offer the disk in good faith – or as an incentive to influence the selection decision? You should state your concerns clearly about this. If the partner knowingly takes advantage of unethically-obtained information, and expects you to be silent about it, you are being made party to an unethical course of action; this is a serious ethical conflict, and you should get confidential independent advice on how to deal with it.

➡️ **Signpost**

See the AAT Code of Professional Ethics:

- **Section 310**: Potential conflicts
- **Section 100**: Ethical conflict resolution (100.18 – 100.23)

DEALING WITH ILLEGAL OR UNETHICAL CONDUCT BY AN EMPLOYER

In addition to ethical conflicts directly affecting your own work, you may become aware that your employers have committed (or may be about to commit) an act that you believe to be illegal or unethical.

Examples include:

- Various forms of **fraud**

- **Falsification of records**, or the supply of information or statements that are false or misleading

- The **offer of inducements** to influence external parties (such as government officials) who have power to help or hinder the employer's operations. This may take the form of bribes (payments made to secure services to which a company is not legally entitled) or 'grease money' (payments made to speed up services that are being stalled or obstructed). 'Gifts' are more problematical (particularly in some cultures, where they are regarded as part of civilised negotiation), but they are unethical if their intent is to influence decisions in the company's favour (eg to win a contract).

- The **acceptance of inducements** to help or hinder the interests of others, or to compromise objectivity and impartiality. For example, clients may offer inducements to collude in fraud or money-laundering, to overlook financial irregularities and so on.

- Other **illegal activity** – from health and safety violations, to money-laundering, to breach of copyright, sexual discrimination or misuse of personal data.

Your aim in dealing with such a situation is, initially, to persuade your employer not to initiate or complete the act, or to put things right and/or to change its policies and controls to ensure that the problem does not occur again. There may be specific machinery to facilitate this process, or you may have to report the matter to successive levels of management with the power of decision-making in relevant areas.

There may be an Ethics Committee in the organisation: a group of executives (perhaps including non-executive directors) appointed to oversee company ethics and to make rulings on allegations of misconduct.

BPP
LEARNING MEDIA

HOW IT WORKS

A payroll clerk at your company approaches you and asks if you can give her some personal advice. You say that you will try to help – if you can – on the understanding that you cannot take responsibility.

It appears that the production department has been tipped off that a Health and Safety Inspector will be visiting the factory in a couple of days, following a complaint. Apparently, the factory supervisors are busy replacing safety guards on machinery, and covering up torn flooring – and generally disguising potential safety hazards. Now the production manager has asked the payroll clerk for a management report on sickness and injury pay, but the specific parameters he has set for the information will make it look as if there have been fewer and less serious accidents than has in fact been the case.

At this point, you stop the clerk and say that it would be inappropriate for you to hear more, but in your opinion this may be a genuine ethical conflict (if all the facts are true), as she is apparently being asked knowingly to present a misleading report. You advise her to speak in the first instance to her own supervisor, stating her concerns and asking the supervisor to take the matter up with the production manager.

Whistle blowing

Whistle blowing is the disclosure by an employee of illegal or unethical practices by his or her employer. Theoretically, this ought to be welcomed as in the public interest – but remember: **confidentiality** is also a very strong value in the accountant's code of ethics.

This is an important issue, because:

(a) You are in a position to uncover information that you may feel requires disclosure.

(b) You may be the one who is given information by a concerned employee or whistleblower.

The Public Interest Disclosure Act

The Nolan Committee on Standards in Public Life, which we discussed in Chapter 1, made the following comments on 'whistle blowing':

"All organisations face the risk of things going wrong or of unknowingly harbouring malpractice ... Encouraging a culture of openness within an organisation will help: prevention is better than cure. Yet it is striking that in the few cases where things have gone badly wrong in local public spending bodies, it has frequently been the tip-off to the press or the local MP ... which has prompted the regulators into action. Placing staff in a position where they feel

driven to approach the media to ventilate concerns is unsatisfactory both for the staff member and the organisation."

In the UK, the **Public Interest Disclosure Act 1998** is part of employment legislation and offers some protection to employees in the private, public and voluntary sectors, ensuring that they cannot suffer detriment for disclosing otherwise confidential information, or to an appropriate regulator, if they do so in good faith and have reasonable grounds to believe:

- That **civil, criminal, regulatory or administrative law** is being breached or is likely to be breached

- That the **health or safety** of any individual has been, is being or is likely to be endangered

- That the **environment** has been, is being or is likely to be damaged and/or

- That **information** on any of the above has been, is being or is likely to be deliberately concealed

The background to the Act was a spate of scandals and disasters in the 1980s and 1990s in the UK, where almost every public enquiry found that workers had been aware of dangers but had either been too scared to raise the alarm, or had raised the matter in the wrong way or with the wrong person.

The Act sets out the circumstances where the disclosure of malpractice outside the organisation is in the public interest and should be protected. The question of whether particular information may, regardless of confidentiality, lawfully be disclosed in the public interest will always need to be carefully considered.

For a disclosure to be protected:

(a) The whistle blower must make the disclosure honestly.

(b) For external disclosures, there must be a substantive basis for the belief that there is malpractice.

(c) For wider public disclosures, the concern should be raised internally first.

Where a whistle blower is victimised or dismissed, he can bring a claim for damages to an employment tribunal.

Confidentiality or 'gagging' clauses in employment contracts and severance agreements (that stop an employee from speaking out) are void if they conflict with the protection given by the Act.

The most ethical approach may be to encourage and use available lines of communication within the company – so that there is less need to whistle blow externally.

BPP
LEARNING MEDIA

Task 5

You work in a large accounting practice. If you begin to suspect that your manager is using his position in your organisation to launder money, who should you report this to?

	✓
SOCA	
The Police	
Your firm's MLRO (providing they are not your manager)	

 Signpost

See the AAT's separate guidance notes on whistle blowing available from its website www.aat.org.uk:

- *The ethics of whistle blowing*

CHAPTER OVERVIEW

- Generally speaking, ethical conduct is **legal conduct**.

- When making an ethical decision, it can help to (i) consider the **consequences** and (ii) consider your own **obligations**.

- A **basic test** is to consider whether you want to be on the receiving end of whatever action you are about to take.

- If you are employed by an organisation, any matter of ethical concern should be raised with your **immediate supervisor**. If you are self-employed, you may need to seek **independent advice**.

- The **AAT's Ethics Advice Line** is also available.

- Particular ethical issues are raised by performing **taxation services**. When you submit a tax return or computations for a client or employer, you are acting as an agent of the taxpayer.

- You have a **duty** to put forward the best position, in favour of your employer or client. You also have a duty towards the tax authorities to provide information in good faith.

- As an accountant you are required to be vigilant for instances of **money laundering** – the attempt to conceal the identity of money created as a consequence of illegal activities.

- In any **conflict of loyalties**, the requirements of the law and your professional standards take precedence – although you should use your judgement as to whether they will be seriously compromised enough to take action through grievance or ethics procedures.

- **Not everyone thinks alike on ethical matters**; it is quite possible that a colleague will honestly disagree with you about what constitutes an ethical or unethical course of action.

- If you are asked, instructed or encouraged to take a course of action that is illegal, or unethical by the standards of your profession, you are **entitled and required to refuse**.

- If you suspect that your employers have committed or may commit an illegal or significant unethical act, your first aim is to persuade them to stop or to put the matter right. If they do not, you may have to make a **disclosure** to an appropriate regulator – but you should seek **independent legal advice**.

- **Whistle blowing** is the disclosure by an employee of illegal or unethical practices by his or her employer. Employees are protected from detriment by the **Public Interest Disclosure Act**.

TEST YOUR LEARNING

Respond to the following by selecting the appropriate option.

Test 1

A self-employed AAT member with an ethical dilemma should seek advice from:

	✓
An independent legal expert or an employee with ethics training	
The AAT Ethics Advice line or a close friend	
An independent legal expert or the AAT Ethics Advice line	

Test 2

You have a duty towards the tax authorities to

	✓
Provide information in good faith.	
Put forward the best possible position for the client on the basis of the information they provide you.	

Test 3

HMRC has extensive legal power to:

	✓
Compel an accountant to cease to act for a client.	
Prosecute a tax agent for failing to get the best possible refund for his or her client.	
Obtain information that may otherwise be withheld.	

Test 4

If you are an employed member of a professional body you owe a duty of loyalty to

	✓
The AAT and HMRC	
Your employer and your client	
Your employer and your profession	

Test 5

The maximum period of imprisonment for committing the offence of tipping off is

	✓
Five years	
Seven years	
Fourteen years	

Test 6

In a self-employed situation, if a client requests or instructs you to take a course of action that is unethical or illegal, you are entitled and required in the first instance to

	✓
Terminate the appointment at once.	
Refuse.	
Report your client to the relevant authorities.	

Test 7

The Public Interest Disclosure Act 1998

	✓
Protects employees from being dismissed for public disclosures if they act in good faith	
Ensures that employees who whistle blow will be dismissed if they act outside the public interest	
Protects employees from suffering detriment for internal whistle blowing, or reporting to a regulator, in good faith	

BPP LEARNING MEDIA

ANSWERS TO CHAPTER TASKS

CHAPTER 1 – The principles of ethical working

1   This is personal to you, so that you begin to think about your own assumptions and beliefs about what kinds of behaviour are 'OK' and 'not OK'. Some of these may be in line with the ethical values of the AAT and accounting profession (such as being honest, telling the truth, being fair and working hard) and some may not be (such as using your work position for the benefit of family members, or offering gifts as a smoother of business relationships and negotiations). In a way, these instances – where your values differ from the professional standards – are more useful information: you know where your 'blind spots' are, and where you may have to modify your assumptions and habits.

2   The correct answer is:

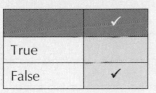

	✓
True	
False	✓

Straightforwardness and honesty are related to the fundamental principle of integrity.

3   Continuing professional development (CPD) is important to accountancy professionals as it helps them **maintain** competency in their role.

Accountancy professionals attain competence by passing professional exams and gaining relevant experience. It is the *maintenance* of professional competence that requires continuing awareness and understanding of relevant technical, professional and business developments and is achieved through CPD.

4 The correct answer is:

	✓
If they are asked for during legal proceedings	✓
When your manager tells you to disclose the information	
When writing a report for general circulation within your organisation	

In this case you have a legal duty to disclose the information.

5 The correct answer is:

	✓
Self-interest	
Advocacy	
Intimidation	✓

'Significant pressure' indicates intimidation threat.

6 The correct answer is:

	✓
The Financial Reporting Review Panel	
The Accounting Standards Board	
The Professional Oversight Board	✓

The Professional Oversight Board (POB) acts as an independent body responsible for monitoring the regulation of the accountancy profession by the professional accountancy bodies.

7 The correct answer is:

	✓
Independence	
Openness	✓
Confidentiality	

Openness is a principle identified by the Nolan Committee.

8   The correct answer is:

	✓
Reputational	
Litigation	
Physical	✓

Damage to assets is a loss which results from physical risk.

9   The correct answer is:

	✓
Annually	
Twice a year	✓

AAT members in practice have to complete the AAT CPD cycle twice a year.

10   The correct answer is:

	✓
True	
False	✓

The AAT's Code does not have the force of law.

CHAPTER 2 – Behaving in an ethical manner I

1   The examples you come up with will be relevant to you or your work. However, some examples of common dishonest behaviour include:

- Stealing property

- Using company information for person gain

- Knowingly selling products with defects

- Damage to physical assets – vandalism

- Using pirated software

- Deliberately producing inaccurate or misleading information

2   The correct answer is:

	✔
Self-review	✔
Intimidation	
Advocacy	

According to the AAT's *Code of Professional Ethics*, a member of an assurance (audit) team who has recently been an officer or director of the client is an example of a self-review threat.

3   The correct answer is:

	✔
How profitable the relationship will be	
Whether acceptance would create any threats to compliance with the fundamental principles	✔
Whether the client's directors meet the firm's moral and ethical standards	

Whilst the client's profitability and ethical standards may be considered by the firm, the AAT's Code does not require them to be considered.

BPP
LEARNING MEDIA

4   The correct answer is:

	✓
True	✓
False	

The situation might arise where the accountant has to act for one of the clients to the detriment of the other.

5   The correct answer is:

	✓
True	
False	✓

Low fees are permitted providing a quality service can be provided at that price. However the statement goes on to make a disparaging remark about the competition which is contrary to the AAT's *Code of Professional Ethics*.

CHAPTER 3 – Behaving in an ethical manner II

1   The correct answer is:

	✓
Independence of mind	
Independence in appearance	✓
Being independent	

2   Whether it is an ethical issue depends on a number of factors, such as:

The value of the hospitality: a sporting event would not normally be regarded as significant – but it would depend on how lavish the package was (or how rare the tickets).

The circumstances: in this case, the fact that the host is bidding for a major contract might suggest an attempt to influence the decision.

In this case, there is probably no ethical issue for you as you are not the one with the authority to make the decision.

However, due to the fact the tickets are likely to be in high demand and have a high value, and the circumstances, it is likely to be an issue for your manager.

3   Section 4 of the Fraud Act 2006 covers fraud by $\boxed{\text{abuse}}$ of position.

4   The Information Commissioner's Office (ICO) maintains a public register of data controllers. If any part of a data controller's register becomes inaccurate then they should notify the ICO within $\boxed{28}$ days.

5   In the UK claims against an accountant in respect of a simple contract must be brought within $\boxed{6}$ years.

CHAPTER 4 – Taking appropriate action

1   Examples include: health and safety at work; data protection (use of data held by organisations about individuals); equal opportunity and non-discrimination (including avoiding offensive and harassing behaviour towards others on grounds of sex, race and religious beliefs); and company law (e.g. on retention of documents). Plus – of course – not committing common law offences such as theft, fraud or assault!

2   The correct answer is:

	✓
Provide them with a reasonable estimate based on what you achieved last year.	
Tell them that you will save them as much as possible.	
Tell them that you cannot provide such information.	✓

You should not make any statement or promises in this regard, since you are not realistically in a position to do so.

3   The correct answer is:

	✓
Do nothing as admitting errors will damage your professional reputation.	
Correct the error by adjusting this year's tax return to compensate.	
Tell the client to advise HMRC about the error.	✓

Since you acted for the client with regard to the incorrect return, you should advise the client to inform HMRC.

4   The maximum penalty for being found guilty of money laundering is
    14   years in prison.

5   The correct answer is:

	✓
SOCA	
The Police	
Your firm's MLRO (providing they are not your manager)	✓

The guidelines on what to do about this are set out in law and regulations in the UK. In this case, you have a clear duty to 'blow the whistle' to the appropriate internal authority (the MLRO).

BPP
LEARNING MEDIA

TEST YOUR LEARNING – ANSWERS

CHAPTER 1 – The principles of ethical working

1   The correct answer is:

	✓
True	
False	✓

Group values are very important, eg in families and friendship groups (which is where we get our ideas from), national cultures and organisations (which establish ethical norms and expectations by which we have to operate).

2   The correct answer is:

	✓
Enhance the reputation and standing of its members	✓
Limit the number of members that it has	
Make sure that its members are able to earn large salaries	

The AAT needs to protect its reputation and standing by maintaining standards of conduct and service among its members in order to be able to enhance the reputation and standing of its members (so that, for example, they are able to attract and retain clients).

3   The correct answer is:

	✓
Failure to keep up to date on CPD	
A personal financial interest in the client's affairs	✓
Being negligent or reckless with the accuracy of the information provided to the client	

A personal financial interest in the client's affairs will affect objectivity. Failure to keep up to date on CPD is an issue of professional *competence*, while providing inaccurate information reflects upon professional *integrity*.

4   The correct answer is:

	✓
Say that you will get back to him when you have looked up the answer.	
Give him the contact details of a friend in your firm who knows all about accounting standards.	
Clarify the limits of your expertise with the client.	✓

This is an issue of technical competence and due care. You should clarify the limits of your expertise with the client, and *then* seek information or guidance from the relevant source.

5   The correct answer is:

Apply safeguards to eliminate or reduce the threat to an acceptable level.	3
Evaluate the seriousness of the threat.	2
Discontinue the action or relationship giving rise to the threat.	4
Identify a potential threat to a fundamental ethical principle.	1

6   The correct answer is:

	✓
It is in the public interest that employees who fail to comply with standards are prosecuted.	
It is in the public interest that services are carried out to professional standards.	✓

7   The correct answer is:

	✓
Accounting Standards Board	✓
International Federation of Accountants	
Consultative Committee of Accountancy Bodies	
Financial Reporting Review Panel	✓
Professional Oversight Board	✓
Auditing Practices Board	✓
Financial Services Authority	
Accountancy and Actuarial Discipline Board	✓

8   The correct answer is:

	✓
External events	✓
Government regulation	

External events might fall under one of the headings: internal fraud; external fraud; employment practices and workplace safety; clients, products and business practice; damage to physical assets; business disruption and systems failures; processes and delivery of outputs.

9   The correct answer is:

Diplomacy	
Integrity	✓
Honesty	✓
Legality	
Accuracy	
Objectivity	✓
Accountability	✓
Openness	✓

10   The correct answer is:

True	
False	✓

Any fine will be limited to a maximum figure set by the AAT Council.

CHAPTER 2 – Behaving in an ethical manner I

1   The correct answer is:

True	✓
False	

Reliance on safeguards built into a client's system (such as employing competent staff) can be used by an accountant in practice as a safeguard against threats to the fundamental principles (AAT *Code of Professional Ethics* s. 200.17).

2   The correct answer is:

	✓
Self-interest	✓
Self-review	
Advocacy	
Familiarity	
Intimidation	

A self-interest threat is created as you now have an interest in the transaction.

3   The correct answer is:

	✓
Providing a second opinion	✓
Accepting a gift from a supplier	

Providing a second opinion creates a threat to the fundamental principle of professional competence and due care as you may not be aware of all the information you might need to form a second opinion.

4 | The Terrorism Act | forms part of UK anti-money laundering legislation.

Anti-money laundering legislation in the UK consists of the Terrorism Act 2000, the Proceeds of Crime Act 2002, and the Money Laundering Regulations 2007.

CHAPTER 3 – Behaving in an ethical manner II

1   The correct answer is:

	✓
Self-interest	✓
Self-review	
Advocacy	

Accepting gifts and hospitality from a client can give rise to self-interest and intimidation threats to objectivity.

2   Being bribed [is] an offence under the Bribery Act 2010.

The three other offences under this legislation are bribing another person, bribing a foreign public official and failure by a commercial organisation to prevent bribery.

3   The correct answer is:

	✓
True	
False	✓

Clients' monies must be kept separately from monies belonging to the AAT member personally and/or to the practice.

4   The correct answer is:

	✓
True	✓
False	

Failure to notify is an offence under the Data Protection Act.

5   The correct answer is:

[7] years

In the UK, the time limit is six years for actions based on a contract or a claim for civil damages. Six years is therefore the maximum time before which a client could bring legal proceedings, so it is sensible to keep records for a further year to allow time for any action to come to court.

6   The correct answer is:

	✓
True	
False	✓

For example, you cannot claim a lien in relation to the statutory books and accounting records of companies, or over documents that are owned by a third party.

BPP
LEARNING MEDIA

CHAPTER 4 – Taking appropriate action

1   The correct answer is:

	✓
An employee with ethics training	
The AAT Ethics Advice line or a close friend	
An independent legal expert or the AAT Ethics Advice line	✓

Employees or close friends should not be asked due to confidentiality issues.

2   The correct answer is:

	✓
Provide information in good faith.	✓
Put forward the best possible position for the client on the basis of the information they provide you.	

You should only undertake tax work on the understanding that your client or employer will make full and accurate disclosure of the relevant information.

3   The correct answer is:

	✓
Compel an accountant to cease to act for a client.	
Prosecute a tax agent for failing to get the best possible refund for his or her client.	
Obtain information that may otherwise be withheld.	✓

4   The correct answer is:

	✓
The AAT and HMRC	
Your employer and your client	
Your employer and your profession	✓

The AAT Code states: 'A member in business has a responsibility to further the legitimate aims of their employing organisation... [it is also

necessary to] consider circumstances in which conflicts may be created with the duty to comply with the fundamental principles'.

5   The correct answer is:

	✓
Five years	✓
Seven years	
Fourteen years	

The anti-money laundering legislation makes tipping off an offence, the maximum penalty for which is five years imprisonment or an unlimited fine.

6   The correct answer is:

	✓
Terminate the appointment at once.	
Refuse.	✓
Report your client to the relevant authorities.	

The request may have been made in ignorance and good faith, so you should attempt to explain the technical, legal and ethical principles that apply.

7   The correct answer is:

	✓
Protects employees from being dismissed for public disclosures if they act in good faith	
Ensures that employees who whistle blow will be dismissed if they act outside the public interest	
Protects employees from suffering detriment for internal whistle blowing, or reporting to a regulator, in good faith	✓

The whistle blower should have reasonable grounds to believe that a criminal offence has been or will be committed, that the health or safety of any individual is likely to be endangered, that the environment has been, or is being damaged and/or that information on any of the above is being deliberately concealed. Public disclosure is a more complicated situation, requiring legal advice.

BPP
LEARNING MEDIA

Question bank

BPP
LEARNING MEDIA

Chapter 1

Task 1.1

You have recently been helping a corporate client prepare for a takeover of another company. The bid has been a success and the directors of your client are delighted to have acquired this other company at what they consider to be a very good price. In order to thank you for your help in this matter, you and your husband have been offered an all expenses paid week in the company villa in Portugal.

Should you accept this offer or not?

- Yes
- No

Task 1.2

A client of your company has just moved their business to another firm. Some time ago, they requested your manager to send over the client's books and records. He did not. Each time they called to chase up the request, it seems that the manager 'screened' their call and never responded.

What fundamental ethical principle does this situation raise?

- Integrity
- Professional competence and due care
- Professional behaviour

Task 1.3

You work for a firm of chartered accountants and are required to fill out a time sheet to record each hour worked for each client each day. Last Friday you forgot to prepare the sheet for the week, and you are now doing it on Monday morning. However you are not absolutely sure how long you worked for each client on Thursday and Friday as due to pressure of work you did not record it.

What fundamental ethical principle does this situation raise?

- Integrity
- Confidentiality
- Professional behaviour

Task 1.4

While at a party at the weekend, you meet a client of yours who is clearly very concerned about some sales tax issues. You know enough about sales tax to carry out your daily work, but you are not an expert on the areas of imports and exports on which your client is asking your opinion.

What ethical issue does this situation raise?

- Objectivity
- Professional competence and due care
- Professional behaviour

Task 1.5

Which of the following is the best definition of the AAT's Code of Professional Ethics 'conceptual framework'?

- A set of definitions of the fundamental ethical principles

- A problem solving procedure that can be used to give you the best chance of complying with ethical principles

- A set of rules to follow when deciding whether or not to consult the AAT Director of Professional Development

Task 1.6

'As a professional, you should behave with courtesy and consideration towards anyone with whom you come into contact.'

Which of the fundamental ethical principles does this illustrate?

- Integrity
- Professional competence and due care
- Professional behaviour

Task 1.7

You have strong views in support of a client who is being threatened with legal action by a supplier who is alleging late payment of invoices. You have offered to state publicly your views on the matter, in defence of your client.

What type of threat to independence does this situation represent?

- Self-interest threat
- Familiarity threat
- Advocacy threat

....

Task 1.8

Categorise the following safeguards according to whether they are created by the profession, or are present in the work environment by dragging each safeguard to the relevant box:

Profession	Work environment

Drag and drop choices:

Rotation of personnel
Appointment of an ethics officer
Continuing professional development
Corporate governance regulations
Quality controls
Internal audits
Professional standards
Third-party review of financial reports
Mechanisms to protect whistle-blowers

....

BPP LEARNING MEDIA

Task 1.9

A 'rules based' approach to ethical problem solving has the advantage that because things are clear-cut, leaving no room for misunderstanding, it is easier to know what to do.

Which of the following are DISADVANTAGES of such an approach?

- Conflicting interests and priorities must be carefully balanced.

- It sets more rigorous standards of behaviour, and so needs a lot of resources.

- There is a higher risk of getting swamped by the details and missing the bigger picture.

Task 1.10

In the UK, which part of the Financial Reporting Council acts as a tribunal and can impose fines and other sanctions against accountants whose work fails to measure up to professional standards?

- The Accounting Standards Board (ASB)
- The Accountancy and Actuarial Discipline Board (AADB)
- The Professional Oversight Board (POB)

Task 1.11

Complete the following statement by selecting the appropriate word(s) to fill each gap in the sentence:

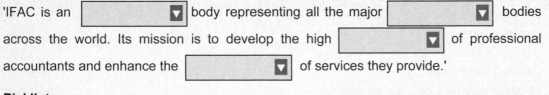

'IFAC is an [____] body representing all the major [____] bodies across the world. Its mission is to develop the high [____] of professional accountants and enhance the [____] of services they provide.'

Picklist

professional
international
cost
standards
accountancy
quality

BPP
LEARNING MEDIA

Task 1.12

Which of the following members of the CCAB is a sponsoring member of the AAT?

- Chartered Accountants Ireland
- ACCA
- CIPFA

Task 1.13

Identify which of the following business values are set out in the Nolan Principles, by dragging only those relevant to the boxes below:

Business values set out in Nolan Principles

Drag and drop options:

Trust
Accountability
Transparency
Accuracy
Selflessness
Honesty

Task 1.14

Monty, a member in practice, performs bookkeeping services for both Stumpy Ltd and Grind Ltd. The companies are in dispute about a series of sales that Stumpy Ltd made to Grind Ltd.

Complete the following sentence by selecting the appropriate option:

'For Monty, this situation threatens the fundamental principles of [_____ ▼]

Picklist

integrity and due care'
confidentiality and professional behaviour'
objectivity and confidentiality'

Task 1.15

What is the name of the body that regulates the financial services industry in the UK?

- The Financial Services Association
- The Financial Services Authority
- The Financial Reporting Council

Task 1.16

Complete the following statement by selecting the appropriate word(s) to fill each gap in the sentence:

'A(n) [▼] is a person who acts as an [▼] between an organisation and the general public.'

'A(n) [▼] is an informal name given to [▼] protection organisations or campaigners.'

Picklist

intermediary
ombudsman
consumer
agent
watchdog
government

Task 1.17

Match the terms by dragging into the appropriate box:

Code of conduct	Code of practice

Drag and drop choices:

Designed to influence the behaviour of employees
Adopted by a profession or organisation to regulate that profession

BPP
LEARNING MEDIA

Task 1.18

Complete the following statement by selecting the appropriate word(s) to fill each gap in the sentence:

The Basel Committee on Banking Supervision (BCBS) defines [▼] risk as:

'The risk of [▼] resulting from inadequate or failed internal [▼],

people and systems or from [▼] events.'

Picklist
International
Operational
Loss
Standards
Processes
External

Task 1.19

John has been found guilty of professional misconduct by an AAT Disciplinary Tribunal.
Which of the following is a possible penalty that he could face?
- Expelled from the Association
- A conviction under criminal law and imprisonment
- Fined an unlimited sum

Task 1.20

Put the AAT's four-stage cycle for CPD under the personal route into order, by dragging the relevant stages to the relevant boxes:

The AAT's four step cycle for CPD under the personal route	
Step 1:	
Step 2:	
Step 3:	
Step 4:	

Drag and drop choices (stages):

Evaluate the outcomes at the year-end
Plan the learning activity you will undertake
Assess your learning and development needs for the year
Put the learning plan into action

Chapter 2

Task 2.1

James, an AAT member in practice, has decided to open his own practice, and as a first marketing step he has decided that his fees will be on average 20% lower than those of his competitors.

What issue does this promotional tool give rise to?

- None – he can charge what he likes.
- It is unethical to charge a lot lower than competitors.
- James should make sure that he can provide a quality service for that price.

Task 2.2

Matt, an AAT member in practice, has been working as a manager on an assurance engagement for an important client of his firm. The engagement is almost at an end and the financial statements will be used by the client's bank to assess whether to increase its lending to the client. The Finance Director of the client has approached Matt and informally discussed the possibility of a high-profile finance position in his department, stating that the role would be his if the assurance report is favourable.

What threats to the fundamental principles of professional ethics does this situation raise?

- Self-review and confidentiality
- Advocacy and self-interest
- Intimidation and self-review
- Self-interest and intimidation
- Advocacy and confidentiality

Task 2.3

Ruchita, an AAT member, wants to offer financial incentives to third parties to introduce clients to her business.

What principles must she adhere to?

- This should not be done at all, as such arrangements are unethical.
- The clients must be made aware of the payments.
- The third party needs to be trusted to carry out the introduction with integrity.
- Ruchita does not have to pay the third party if the client is not a good one.

BPP
LEARNING MEDIA

Task 2.4

Select the most appropriate response from the list:

'In the UK context of the receiving and paying of commissions when introducing clients, the relationship between a client and adviser is regarded as a

▼

Picklist

professional relationship; you must maintain professional standards'

confidential relationship; you cannot divulge any information about commissions paid or received'

fiduciary relationship; you must hand commissions received over to the client'

....

Task 2.5

Complete the following statement by selecting the appropriate word(s) to fill each gap in the sentence:

The [▼] Regulations 2007 require you to exercise 'due diligence' in gathering information about a prospective customer, including:

- The client's [▼], verified by appropriate identification and/or references

- [▼] information, including its expected patterns of business, its business model and its source of funds.

Picklist
Know your client
Money Laundering
confidential
Bribery
acceptable
identity

....

Task 2.6

What does the acronym SOCA stand for?
- Serious Organised Crime Association
- Scene of Crime Authority
- Serious Organised Crime Agency
- Scene of Crime Association

....

Task 2.7

Which of the following pieces of legislation forms part of the anti-money laundering regulations in the UK?

- The Proceeds of Crime Act 2002
- The Fraud Act 2006
- The Public Interest Disclosure Act 1998
- The Bribery Act 2010

Task 2.8

'For existing clients, customer due diligence involves keeping customer due diligence records up to date and undertaking appropriate customer due diligence procedures on any transactions that seem inconsistent with existing knowledge of the client.'

- True
- False

Task 2.9

A client has told you informally that she expects to inherit from a recently deceased relative. You initially declined to advise her informally on tax matters since you were not sure of your expertise. However, she has now received a considerable sum from the relative's estate, and wants to consult you on the best thing for her to do with the money.

What is your position here?

- This amounts to a request for investment advice, and you are not qualified to give it.
- You can give her general advice on what most people do with large inheritances.
- You can point her in the direction of your cousin, who is a financial advisor.

BPP
LEARNING MEDIA

Task 2.10

A client is trying to sell her floristry business, and has asked you to prepare financial statements for the business (income statement, statement of financial position and a 5-year cash flow forecast) for a potential buyer that she has found. She has asked that you base your fee upon the eventual selling price of the business.

What is your position here?

- The fees to prepare the financial statements are permitted under the AAT's Code of Professional Ethics and you can provide the services on the basis suggested.

- You can offer the services on the suggested fee basis, as long as you disclose the fee to the appropriate authority.

- You cannot offer these financial reporting services on the terms suggested as this represents a threat to your objectivity.

Task 2.11

Which of the following services cannot be offered by an accounting technician without relevant authorisation?

- Taxation and insolvency work
- External audits of UK limited companies and taxation work
- Insolvency work and investment business
- Investment business and second opinions

Task 2.12

The AAT Code of Professional Ethics prohibits members from giving second opinions because the threat to the ethical principle of professional competence and due care is too great to be eliminated or reduced to an acceptable level by the application of appropriate safeguards.

- True
- False

Task 2.13

A member of the public has asked you as an AAT member to provide them with a second opinion on advice they have received from another firm. However you will not have access to the books and records the other firm used to prepare their advice because they are still holding onto them.

If you were to provide a second opinion without these books and records then this would be in breach of which fundamental principle?

- Confidentiality
- Professional competence and due care
- Objectivity

Task 2.14

'Pre-arranged fees are not a good idea, as it is impossible to tell what may happen during an assignment.'

- True
- False

Task 2.15

Keith, a member in practice, wishes to enter into a professional relationship with a client.

Answer the following question by selecting the appropriate option:

As part of his customer due diligence processes, which of the following actions must Keith take?

- Verify the validity of the client's business model and cashflow data
- Verify the client's identity
- Notify the FRC of the proposed relationship

BPP
LEARNING MEDIA

Task 2.16

Johnny, an AAT member in practice, has been accused of bringing the profession into disrepute through the marketing of his practice.

Complete the following sentence by selecting the appropriate option:

'This accusation is most likely to be upheld if Johnny:

▼

Picklist

states in an advertisement that he is a fully qualified member of the AAT'

includes his photograph on his letterhead'

makes an uncomplimentary reference in his advertising to the work of a member of the ICAS'

....

Task 2.17

An AAT member can be said to be acting fairly in which of the following circumstances?

- They avoid using their work phone for making personal calls.
- They avoid discriminating against others.
- They respect another's right of confidentiality.

....

Task 2.18

Which of the following represents a self-interest threat for an AAT member in business?

- Having an opportunity to use company assets for own advantage

- Being asked to justify a decision where they were involved in preparing information on which the decision is based

- Having a long association with a business contact

....

Task 2.19

Which of the following represents an advocacy threat to an AAT member in practice?

- Promoting shares in a listed company which they audit
- Depending on a client's fees for a significant portion of their income
- Discovering a significant error when re-evaluating their work

Task 2.20

Bob, a senior AAT member working as a partner in a large practice, has a client who runs a newsagent – but he has heard that another of his clients, a bookshop, is planning to open its own outlet in direct competition. There is clearly going to be a conflict of interest between the two clients.

What should Bob do?

- Inform both clients of the potential for conflict, promise them confidentiality and leave it at that

- No action is required – as a senior member of the practice, Bob is fully aware of the potential for conflicts of interest and will act accordingly

- Propose a 'Chinese wall' by handing the bookshop client to another team at another office; inform both clients of the changes

BPP LEARNING MEDIA

Chapter 3

Task 3.1

Why is professional independence particularly important in assurance services?

- Independence is necessary to enable the member to express a conclusion that is free of bias.

- Independence is necessary to enable the member to charge a realistic fee.

- Independence is necessary to enable the member to gain access to confidential and sensitive information.

Task 3.2

A long association with a business contact, which may influence your decisions, is best described as which type of threat to objectivity and independence?

- Self-interest
- Intimidation
- Familiarity

Task 3.3

Which of the following represents a potential threat to your objectivity?

- Unfamiliar software or systems
- Your uncle is the Finance Director at your main competitor
- Inaccurate information from colleagues when preparing an important report

Task 3.4

Complete the following statement by selecting the appropriate word(s) to fill the gap in the sentence:

'[_____ ▼] are attempts to influence somebody's decisions or actions.'

Picklist
Gifts
Inducements
Offers of hospitality

Task 3.5

What is 'independence of mind'?

- The willingness to avoid situations that could pose questions as to your ability to be objective

- The ability to put aside all considerations that are not relevant to the decision or task at hand

Task 3.6

Choose the most accurate response from the list below:

Serena has been offered a bottle of wine for her wine connoisseur husband as a Christmas gift by a client, in appreciation of her work.

Is she correct to accept the gift?

- Yes – the gift is for her husband, not her
- No – it is never correct to accept gifts from clients
- Yes – the gift is not likely to be perceived as significant enough to affect her objectivity

Task 3.7

Choose the most appropriate responses to complete the sentence below.

The husband of Jessica, a member in practice, has made a large loan to Laing Ltd, where Jessica is currently working on an assurance engagement.

'This situation presents a [▼]

Picklist

familiarity threat
self-interest threat

and the best course of action would be [▼]

Picklist

to remove Jessica from the assurance engagement'
to inform the audit committee of Laing Ltd'

Task 3.8

Fill in the blank by selecting the appropriate option:

If you are employed by a public body in the UK, the acceptance of gifts may be illegal under [▼]

Picklist

AAT's Code of Professional Ethics
The Bribery Act 2010
The Nolan principles

Task 3.9

Under the Fraud Act 2006 a person found guilty of fraud can be punished by a prison sentence or an unlimited fine.

* True
* False

Task 3.10

Sarah, an AAT member working in a manufacturing company, has been asked to prepare detailed financial information on a new product of which she has very little knowledge. The accountant who normally deals with this product is away on leave for several weeks, and the information is required urgently as part of a report to shareholders. Sarah is very unsure about her ability to complete the work to her usual high standards.

What should she do in this situation?

* Take on the challenge, and use the opportunity to impress her colleagues

* Let her manager know that the task is outside the boundaries of her expertise and experience

* Ask for all the information that is available on the new product and ask her friend in another company to do it for her

---

Task 3.11

Robert, an AAT member, holds a number of shares in his employing company, and has become eligible for a profit-related bonus for the first time.

What type of threat could this represent to his objectivity when preparing company financial statements?

- Self-interest
- Self-review
- Intimidation

Task 3.12

Complete the following statement by selecting the appropriate word(s) to fill the gaps in the sentence:

When preparing financial statements, there is a clear need to apply the principles of

[▼] (not disclosing sensitive information), [▼] (preparing and presenting information in accordance with financial reporting and other applicable professional standards) and [▼] (presenting information free of bias or self interest).

Picklist

Objectivity
Professional competence and due care
Confidentiality

Task 3.13

A new client has asked you to hold a significant amount of money but has declined to tell you what the purpose of this money is.

Would you accept this money?

- Yes; it must be held in a separate bank account

- No; you do not know the purpose of the funds

- No; you cannot accept monies from new clients until they have been with you for more than two years

BPP LEARNING MEDIA

Task 3.14

Glen, an AAT member, has just started his own tax advisory business. One of his clients, Joanne, has asked him to keep custody of £25,000 in cash for one month, when it will need to be paid to HM Revenue and Customs.

What should Glen do?

- Hold the money separately from that of his business
- Inform Joanne that he cannot hold the money
- Keep a note of the amount of money, but hold it in his established bank account

Task 3.15

Gregory is an AAT member in practice who acts as account signatory on behalf of a client, Natalie, who is frequently out of the country and non-contactable on long business trips. Last month Greg transferred £7,000 to himself from one of Natalie's many bank accounts.

Answer the following question by selecting the appropriate option:

Which Fraud Act 2006 offence is it most likely that Gregory has committed?

- Fraud by false representation
- Fraud by failing to disclose information
- Fraud by abuse of position

Task 3.16

Saskia is an AAT member in practice, employed by Evans LLP. She has recently completed an assurance engagement at Lawrence Ltd. Lawrence Ltd is no longer a client of Evans LLP, but Saskia has acquired some information about it that would be of interest to another client, DH Ltd.

Complete the following sentence by selecting the appropriate option from the dropdown menu:

'The principle of confidentiality [▼]

Picklist

imposes an obligation on Saskia not to disclose the information to DH Ltd'
imposes no obligation on Saskia: Lawrence Ltd is no longer a client'
imposes an obligation on Saskia, but her assistant is free to disclose'

Task 3.17

Paul is an AAT member who acts as a principal in relation to his client, Sue Ltd. Paul has agreed to prepare the payables ledger control account reconciliation as a one-off service to assist with the year end procedures.

Complete the following sentence by selecting the appropriate option:

'Ownership of the reconciliation when it is complete is [▼]

Picklist

Paul's'
Sue Ltd's'

Task 3.18

Peter is an AAT member who acts as a principal in relation to his client, Mary Ltd. Peter has been involved in lengthy correspondence with Jones Ltd, regarding consultancy work that Jones Ltd undertook for Mary Ltd, and which Peter is investigating.

Complete the following sentence by selecting the appropriate option:

'Ownership of this correspondence with Jones Ltd belongs to [▼]

Picklist

Peter'
Mary Ltd'

BPP
LEARNING MEDIA

Task 3.19

Identify the three conditions that must exist for John, an AAT member, to have a right of lien over the documents of his client, Elton Ltd. Drag and drop the three valid conditions into the table below:

A right of lien exists when the following conditions apply:

Drag and drop options (conditions):

The documents belong to Elton Ltd.
The documents are Elton Ltd's statutory books and accounting records.
The documents are in John's possession because he has been working on them.
The documents are being held by John after being left at his office by Elton Ltd by mistake .
Work has been done by John on the documents and the fee has been paid.
Work has been done by John on the documents, but the fee is outstanding.

Task 3.20

Complete the following sentence by selecting the appropriate option:

Failure by a member in practice of the duty to exercise reasonable care and skill means the member may be liable for [▼]

Picklist

fraud, leading to a claim for compensation
professional negligence, leading to a claim for damages
breach of duty of care, and a claim for compensation

Chapter 4

Task 4.1

If you are employed by an organisation, where should you take any ethical concerns in the first instance if you cannot resolve them with the other person concerned?

- Your immediate supervisor as part of an ethical reporting procedure
- The AAT Ethics Advice Line
- An independent legal expert

Task 4.2

Fill in the blank by selecting the appropriate option:

When you submit a tax return or computations for a client or employer, you are acting as [　　　　　▼] of the taxpayer.

Picklist

principal
agent

Task 4.3

Fill in the blank by selecting the appropriate option:

Fred, an AAT member, is preparing tax computations for his client, Barney Ltd. It is [　　　　　▼] who bears ultimate responsibility for the accuracy of the data and computations.

Picklist

Barney Ltd
Fred

BPP
LEARNING MEDIA

Task 4.4

Pat, an AAT member in practice, has become aware of a significant error in a tax return from a previous year for one of her clients, Connor Ltd.

What should she do?

- Immediately advise Connor Ltd – and recommend that they inform HMRC
- Make the disclosure herself
- Resign from the appointment

Task 4.5

Under-declaring income and over-declaring expenses on a tax computation can lead to accusations of money laundering.

- True
- False

Task 4.6

Sam, an AAT member, has misgivings over one of his clients, Avalon Ltd. He believes that there is undeclared income and has asked the owners to supply him with a general assurance, in writing, that all income is being declared. It is now time to prepare Avalon Ltd's tax return.

How should Sam approach his next meeting with the client?

- Assure them that he is 'on their side' and will get them the best tax refund that he possibly can

- Ensure that they understand that they bear ultimate responsibility for the accuracy of the facts, information and tax computations, and that he can refuse to be associated with their tax return if he suspects that it is incomplete or inaccurate

- Tell them that he cannot act for them any more as he believes that they are not declaring their full income

Task 4.7

When an AAT member faces a conflict between professional standards and his or her duty towards an employer (for example if the employer asks that a misleading tax return be submitted), what should take priority?

- The rules and standards of the profession take priority
- The employer's objectives should be put first

Task 4.8

Fill in the blank:

While an AAT member may seek independent or professional advice on an ethical matter, he or she is still bound by a duty of [▼]

Picklist

confidentiality
competence
co-operation

Task 4.9

For a member in practice, if a client requests or instructs you to take a course of action that is unethical or illegal, what should you do?

- Refuse to take that course of action
- Immediately cease to act for that client

Task 4.10

Jimmy, an AAT member, has been employed for some years by Laura LLP. He feels that his department manager Nadia poses a threat to his ability to perform his duties with the appropriate degree of professional behaviour, as she keeps asking him to falsify his timesheets so that she can charge higher fees to clients. Jimmy wishes to make a disclosure to senior management at Laura LLP.

Answer the following question by selecting the appropriate option:

What is Jimmy's position as a whistle-blower in relation to the Public Interest Disclosure Act 1998?

- He will be protected provided he acts in good faith
- He will not be protected unless he discloses to a legal adviser
- He will not be protected as this is a breach of confidentiality

---

Task 4.11

Answer the following question by selecting the appropriate option:

Which of the following disclosures does the Public Interest Disclosure Act 1998 cover?

- Professional negligence
- Endangerment of an individual's health and safety
- Breach of contract

BPP
LEARNING MEDIA

Task 4.12

Savya is an AAT member on an assurance engagement at Paint plc. During the course of the engagement he has heard client staff talking about certain funds, which Savya now believes derive from tax evasion.

Complete the following sentence by selecting the appropriate option:

'Savya must report his suspicions so as to avoid a charge of [▼]

Picklist

Professional negligence'
Failure to report'
Breach of confidentiality'

··

Task 4.13

Why should written records be kept of discussions and meetings on ethical issues?

- To avoid allegations of professional misconduct
- To ensure that there is evidence of any advice received
- To send to the AAT Director of Professional Development

··

Task 4.14

Wilma, an AAT member, is leaving her employment with Betty Ltd after a disagreement with her manager over his handling of a bad working relationship with a colleague in the sales department. She has made the reasons for her resignation clear to her employer in her exit interview, and she wants to go to the local newspaper about what she sees as Betty Ltd's failure to listen to her concerns.

What is Wilma's position?

- Wilma is bound by a duty of confidentiality not to talk about her reasons for leaving.
- Wilma is entitled to talk to the local paper about her treatment by Betty Ltd.
- Wilma can sue Betty Ltd for breach of contract.

··

Task 4.15

What two factors need to be balanced when considering whether or not to 'blow the whistle'?

- Confidentiality and objectivity
- Competence and public interest
- Confidentiality and public interest
- Duty of care and confidentiality

Task 4.16

Susie, an AAT member employed by Luna plc, is facing significant pressure from her manager to give incorrect information to the company's internal auditors.

Complete the following sentence by selecting the appropriate option from each dropdown menu:

'Susie's situation represents [▼]

Picklist

an intimidation threat
an advocacy threat

and her immediate response should be to implement the safeguard of

Picklist

obtaining advice from the AAT'
refusing to co-operate with the internal audit'

Task 4.17

You are aware that the retail company that you work for has taken on a full time sales person for its new shop, but when checking the payroll records you can find no mention of this new employee, nor any payments to her.

What is the first thing that you should do in this situation?

- Nothing – the arrangements between the shop and the employee are not your responsibility

- Speak to the payroll department, warning them about the risks of payroll fraud

- Speak to your manager

BPP
LEARNING MEDIA

Task 4.18

Arousha, an AAT member, has been asked by her boss to include information in an important report to the Board of Directors that she knows to be inaccurate.

What type of threat does this represent, and what should she do as a first step?

- Intimidation threat; seek legal advice
- Self-review threat; resign
- Intimidation threat; refuse to be associated with the information
- Self-review threat; seek legal advice

Task 4.19

Which of the following constitutes money laundering?

- Benefits obtained through bribery
- Delaying payments to suppliers for as long as possible
- Using of client money to pay outstanding fees

Task 4.20

What is 'tipping off'?

- Disclosing something that might prejudice an investigation
- Advising clients on the prevention of money laundering
- Disclosing suspicion of money laundering activity to the appropriate authorities

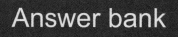

Answer bank

BPP
LEARNING MEDIA

Answer bank

Chapter 1

Task 1.1

The correct answer is: No.

This offer of a free holiday should not be accepted due to the principles of professional behaviour and objectivity. The offer is of significant value. Such a gift, if accepted, could be seen from an observer's point of view as payment in kind for special favours, or may indicate that you may be biased towards that client in future.

Task 1.2

The correct answer is: Professional behaviour

This is simply unprofessional behaviour by your manager. You may consider reporting the matter to your in-house ethics committee, if there is one.

Task 1.3

The correct answer is: Integrity

From a personal point of view this is a matter of integrity. Your clients are charged fees on the basis of the hours that you and other members of the firm work for them, so it is important that the recording of these hours is accurate. Therefore you are right to be concerned about not knowing the precise hours, and should ensure that this situation does not happen again.

Task 1.4

The correct answer is: Professional competence and due care

This raises issues of professional competence and due care. You know that you do not have the knowledge to answer these questions at this time and in this situation. For your own professional safety, you should make the client clearly aware of this and not be prepared to give any opinion, as this may be relied upon by the client despite the circumstances. The most appropriate form of action would be to make an appointment with the client to discuss the matter properly after you have done some research into these specific areas, or refer them to a colleague with experience in this area.

Task 1.5

The correct answer is:

A problem solving procedure that can be used to give you the best chance of complying with ethical principles.

Task 1.6

The correct answer is: Professional behaviour.

'The principle of professional behaviour imposes an obligation on members to comply with relevant laws and regulations and avoid any action that may bring disrepute to the profession.'

Task 1.7

The correct answer is: Advocacy threat.

The risk is that, since you are prepared to promote your opinion, people will have difficulty in believing that you are objective.

Task 1.8

Profession	Work environment
Continuing professional development	Quality controls
Corporate governance regulations	Internal audits
Professional standards	Mechanisms to protect whistle-blowers
Third-party review of financial reports	Rotation of personnel
	Appointment of an ethics officer

Task 1.9

The correct answer is:

There is a higher risk of getting swamped by the details and missing the bigger picture.

BPP
LEARNING MEDIA

Tasks 1.10

The correct answer is: The Accountancy and Actuarial Discipline Board (AADB)

Tasks 1.11

'IFAC is an | international | body representing all the major **accountancy** bodies across the world. Its mission is to develop the high | standards | of professional accountants and enhance the | quality | of services they provide.'

Task 1.12

The correct answer is: CIPFA

Task 1.13

The correct answer is:

Business values set out in Nolan Principles
Accountability
Selflessness
Honesty

Task 1.14

The correct answer is:

For Monty, this situation threatens the fundamental principles of | objectivity and confidentiality |

Task 1.15

The correct answer is: The Financial Services Authority

Task 1.16

The correct answer is:

'An ⟨ombudsman⟩ is a person who acts as an ⟨intermediary⟩ between an organisation and the general public.'

'A ⟨watchdog⟩ is an informal name given to ⟨consumer⟩ protection organisations or campaigners.'

Task 1.17

The correct answer is:

Code of conduct	Code of practice
Designed to influence the behaviour of employees	Adopted by a profession or organisation to regulate that profession

Task 1.18

The correct answer is:

The Basel Committee on Banking Supervision (BCBS) defines ⟨operational⟩ risk as: 'The risk of ⟨loss⟩ resulting from inadequate or failed internal ⟨processes⟩, people and systems or from ⟨external⟩ events.'

Task 1.19

The correct answer is: Expelled from the Association.

John may be expelled from the Association. There cannot be a criminal conviction as failing to follow the AAT's Code of Professional Ethics is not a criminal offence. He may be fined, but there is a maximum amount which is set by the council so it cannot be unlimited.

Task 1.20

The correct answer is:

The AAT's four step cycle for CPD under the personal route	
Step 1:	Assess your learning and development needs for the year
Step 2:	Plan the learning activity you will undertake
Step 3:	Put the learning plan into action
Step 4:	Evaluate the outcomes at the year-end

Chapter 2

Task 2.1

The correct answer is: James should make sure that he can provide a quality service for that price.

If fees are mentioned in promotional material, James must ensure that the statements are not misleading, e.g. about what is covered and how the fees are calculated.

....

Task 2.2

The correct answer is: Self-interest and intimidation

....

Task 2.3

The correct answers are:

- The clients must be made aware of the payments.
- The third party needs to be trusted to carry out the introduction with integrity.

....

Task 2.4

The correct answer is: Fiduciary relationship; you must hand commissions received over to the client.

In the UK, if you receive a commission for introducing a client to another firm, and you are the client's professional adviser (regarded in UK law as a 'fiduciary relationship'), you are legally bound to hand the money over to the client – unless they specifically approve your keeping it.

....

Task 2.5

The correct answer is:

The Money Laundering Regulations 2007 require you to exercise 'due diligence' in gathering information about a prospective customer, including:

- The client's identity , verified by appropriate identification and/or references.

- Know your client information, including its expected patterns of business, its business model and its source of funds.

....

Task 2.6

The correct answer is: Serious Organised Crime Agency

Task 2.7

The correct answer is: The Proceeds of Crime Act 2002

Task 2.8

The correct answer is: True

Task 2.9

The correct answer is: This amounts to a request for investment advice, and you are not qualified to give it.

Task 2.10

The correct answer is: You cannot offer these financial reporting services on the terms suggested as this represents a threat to your objectivity.

Fees that depend on the outcome of an assignment are known as contingency fees and they must not be charged for financial reporting services as in this example.

Task 2.11

The correct answer is: Insolvency work and investment business

Accounting technicians must also not carry out the external audits of UK limited companies and the provision of corporate financial advice, without the relevant authorisation.

Task 2.12

The correct answer is: False

The AAT Code of Professional Ethics does not prohibit members from providing second opinions, provided that appropriate safeguards can be applied to eliminate or reduce significant threats to an acceptable level.

....

Task 2.13

The correct answer is: Professional competence and due care.

Professional competence is at risk if you do not base your opinion on the same set of facts as the other accountant or if you have insufficient evidence to make a decision.

....

Task 2.14

The correct answer is: False. Pre-arranged fees are quite acceptable, as long as the fee is fair for the work – and the work is fulfilled on that basis.

....

Task 2.15

The correct answer is: Verify the client's identity.

Accountants should verify the identity of any new clients.

....

Task 2.16

The correct answer is:

'This accusation is most likely to be upheld if Johnny

| makes an uncomplimentary reference in his advertising to the work of a member of the ICAS.' |

Members must never make disparaging references to, or comparisons with, the practice or services of others.

....

Task 2.17

The correct answer is: They avoid discriminating against others.

Not using a work phone for personal calls is an example of being honest. Respecting another's right to confidentiality is an example of sensitivity.

Task 2.18

The correct answer is: Having an opportunity to use company assets for own advantage

Being asked to justify a decision where they were involved in preparing information on which the decision is based is an example of a self-review threat.

Having a long association with a business contact can create a familiarity threat.

Task 2.19

The correct answer is: Promoting shares in a listed company which they audit.

- Depending on a client's fees for a significant portion of their income is an example of a self-interest threat.

- Discovering a significant error when re-evaluating their work is an example of a self-review threat.

Task 2.20

The correct answer is: Propose a 'Chinese wall' by handing the bookshop client to another team at another office; inform both clients of the changes.

It may also be prudent to insert a paragraph into new engagement letters, stating that 'all information will be kept confidential, except as required by law, regulatory or ethical guidance, and the client permits the firm to take such steps as the firm thinks fit to preserve confidentiality.'

BPP
LEARNING MEDIA

Chapter 3

Task 3.1

The correct answer is: Independence is necessary to enable the member to express a conclusion that is free of bias.

Task 3.2

The correct answer is: Familiarity

Task 3.3

The correct answer is: Your uncle is the Finance Director at your main competitor

Your uncle being the competitor's Finance Director is more likely to be a threat to your *objectivity*. All of the other options represent potential threats to professional competence.

Task 3.4

The correct answer is: ' Inducements are attempts to influence somebody's decisions or actions.'

Inducements may be made to encourage dishonest behaviour or to gain confidential information.

Task 3.5

The correct answer is: The ability to put aside all considerations that are not relevant to the decision or task at hand.

This is, essentially, objectivity – free from bias, prejudice or partiality.

Task 3.6

The correct answer is: Yes – the gift is not likely to be perceived as significant enough to affect her objectivity.

Task 3.7

The correct answer is:

'This situation presents a self-interest threat and the best course of action would be to remove Jessica from the assurance engagement'.

Task 3.8

The correct answer is:

If you are employed by a public body in the UK, the acceptance of gifts may be illegal under the Bribery Act 2010.

Task 3.9

The correct answer is: True

Fraud is a criminal offence punishable by imprisonment or an unlimited fine.

Task 3.10

The correct answer is: Let her manager know that the task is outside the boundaries of her expertise and experience.

It is important to be realistic and responsible and let people know when you are not confident about completing a task, especially when it is a significant one.

Task 3.11

The correct answer is: Self-interest.

If such threats are significant (i.e. the interest is direct and of high value), safeguards will have to be put in place.

Task 3.12

The correct answer is:

When preparing financial statements, there is a clear need to apply the principles of confidentiality (not disclosing sensitive information), professional competence and due care (preparing and presenting information in accordance with financial reporting and other applicable professional standards) and objectivity (presenting information free of bias or self-interest).

Task 3.13

The correct answer is: No; you do not know the purpose of the funds.

In this case you cannot accept the monies, as you cannot hold clients' monies without verifying the commercial purpose of the transaction.

Task 3.14

The correct answer is: Hold the money separately from that of his business.

Clients' monies should be kept separately from monies belonging to the member personally and/or to the practice.

Task 3.15

The correct answer is: Fraud by abuse of position

Task 3.16

The correct answer is:

The principle of confidentiality imposes an obligation on Saskia not to disclose the information to DH Ltd.

It applies even after the assignment, or the contractual relationship with the client is over. It applies not just to members, but also to any staff under their supervision.

Task 3.17

The correct answer is:

'Ownership of the reconciliation when it is complete is [Sue Ltd's].'

Documents that have been created by a principal on the specific instructions of the client belong to the client.

Task 3.18

The correct answer is:

'Ownership of this correspondence with Jones Ltd belongs to [Peter],

Letters exchanged with third parties belong to the principal.

Task 3.19

The correct answer is:

A right of lien exists when the following conditions apply:
The documents belong to Elton Ltd.
The documents are in John's possession because he has been working on them.
Work has been done by John on the documents, but the fee is outstanding.

Task 3.20

Failure by a member in practice of the duty to exercise reasonable care and skill means the member may be liable for [professional negligence, leading to a claim for damages]

BPP
LEARNING MEDIA

Chapter 4

Task 4.1

The correct answer is:

Your immediate supervisor as part of an ethical reporting procedure.

....

Task 4.2

The correct answer is:

When you submit a tax return or computations for a client or employer, you are acting as an ⬚ agent ⬚ of the taxpayer.

....

Task 4.3

The correct answer is:

Fred, an AAT member, is preparing tax computations for his client, Barney Ltd. It is ⬚ Barney Ltd ⬚ who bears ultimate responsibility for the accuracy of the data and computations.

....

Task 4.4

The correct answer is: Immediately advise Connor Ltd – and recommend that they inform HMRC.

....

Task 4.5

The correct answer is: True

For the purposes of money laundering provisions, the proceeds of deliberate tax evasion are just as much 'criminal property' as money from drug trafficking or theft.

....

Task 4.6

The correct answer is: Ensure that they understand that they bear ultimate responsibility for the accuracy of the facts, information and tax computations, and that he can refuse to be associated with their tax return if he suspects that it is incomplete or inaccurate.

Task 4.7

The correct answer is: The rules and standards of the profession take priority.

Task 4.8

The correct answer is:

While an AAT member may seek independent or professional advice on an ethical matter, he or she is still bound by a duty of | confidentiality |.

Task 4.9

The correct answer is: Refuse to take that course of action

The member should refuse and perhaps explain the ethical or professional principles involved, in an attempt to get the client to change their mind.

Task 4.10

The correct answer is: He will be protected provided he acts in good faith.

Task 4.11

The correct answer is: Endangerment of an individual's health and safety

Task 4.12

The correct answer is:

'Savya must report his suspicions so as to avoid a charge of | Failure to report |.'

BPP
LEARNING MEDIA

Task 4.13

The correct answer is: To ensure that there is evidence of any advice received.

This will help to protect you in any legal proceedings that may result; if your subsequent conduct is prosecuted, for example – or if you are unfairly victimised or dismissed for taking a stand on the issue.

....

Task 4.14

The correct answer is: Wilma is bound by a duty of confidentiality not to talk about her reasons for leaving.

This is because there does not appear to be any legal duty to disclose what has happened.

....

Task 4.15

The correct answer is: Confidentiality and public interest.

Whistle-blowing is the disclosure by an employee of illegal or unethical practices by his or her employer. This can be in the public interest – but confidentiality is also a very strong value to consider.

....

Task 4.16

The correct answer is:

Susie's situation represents an intimidation threat and her immediate response should be to implement the safeguard of obtaining advice from the AAT .

....

Task 4.17

The correct answer is: Speak to your manager

Your first step is probably to speak to your manager about your concerns, and it may then be suggested that you speak to the payroll department in general terms about the importance of accurate reporting. In this situation you will probably be suspicious that the employee is being paid in cash in order to avoid the tax consequences of employment. Payroll fraud is an offence that is reportable to SOCA.

....

Task 4.18

The correct answer is: Intimidation threat; refuse to be associated with the information

This is an intimidation threat, and as a first step she should refuse to be associated with incorrect information. If her manager persists in his request, Arousha may need to take legal advice.

Task 4.19

The correct answer is: Benefits obtained through bribery

Money laundering is a process by which criminals attempt to conceal the true origin and ownership of the proceeds of their criminal activity.

Task 4.20

The correct answer is: Disclosing something that might prejudice an investigation

BPP
LEARNING MEDIA

AAT PRACTICE ASSESSMENT 1 PROFESSIONAL ETHICS IN ACCOUNTING AND FINANCE

Time allowed: 1 hour 30 minutes

AAT PRACTICE ASSESSMENT 1

The AAT assessment has been updated for the guidance expected to apply to assessments from 1 September 2012.

Section 1

Task 1.1

Complete the following sentences by selecting the appropriate option.

The behaviour of a member who is straightforward and honest in all professional and business relationships is following the fundamental principle of [▼]

Picklist

objectivity
professional competence and due care
integrity

The conceptual framework approach requires members to

[▼]

Picklist

comply with a specific set of rules
identify, evaluate and respond to threats to compliance with the fundamental principles

Task 1.2

Answer the following questions by selecting the appropriate option in each case.

(a) **The accountancy profession is committed to which of the following objectives?**

An outlook which is essentially commercial, achieved by being business minded and free from regulatory pressure. [ ]

Rendering services to acceptable standards of conduct and performance. [ ]

Acknowledgement of duties to society as a whole in addition to duties to the employer or client. [✓]

(b) **In the UK, which part of the Financial Reporting Council has direct responsibility for reviewing the way in which the professional accountancy bodies regulate their members?**

The Accounting Standards Board (ASB) [✓]

The Accountancy and Actuarial Discipline Board (AADB) [ ]

The Professional Oversight Board (POB) [✓]

Complete the following sentence by selecting the appropriate option from the list below.

(c) A code of business ethics in an organisation should be designed to help an individual in the organisation:

▼

Picklist

make the right choice between alternative courses of action

identify the appropriate person to whom an ethical dilemma should be referred

Task 1.3

Identify whether each of the following professional accountancy bodies is or is not a sponsoring body of the AAT by dragging each body in the appropriate box.

Sponsoring body of the AAT	Not a sponsoring body of the AAT
ICAS *~~FRC~~* CIPFA ICAEW CIMA CAI	CAI IFAC IRC ACCA

Drag and drop options:

CAI	IFAC	ICAS	FRC
ICAEW	CIMA	CIPFA	ACCA

Task 1.4

Respond to the following statement by selecting the appropriate option.

(a) **The AAT Code of Professional Ethics is an example of civil law.**

True ☒

False ☑

Answer the following task by selecting the appropriate option.

(b) **Which of the following is a valid reason for an organisation to introduce an ethical code?**

To ensure that there is consistency of conduct by employees across the organisation. ☑

To impose criminal sanctions on employees who fail to comply with the ethical code. ☐

Task 1.5

Complete the following sentence by selecting the appropriate option.

(a) **According to the Basel Committee on Banking Supervision, the definition of operational risk is:**

The risk of direct or indirect loss resulting from inadequate or failed [▼]

Picklist

processes, people and systems

regulation

Answer the following task by selecting the appropriate option.

(b) **Cecily, a member in practice, wishes to enter into a professional relationship with a client which will almost certainly last for at least two years. As part of her customer due diligence processes, which of the following actions must Cecily take?**

Notify the AAT of the relationship. ☐

Verify the nature and value of the client's assets. ☐

Verify the client's identity on the basis of documents, data or other reliable information. ☑

Task 1.6

(a) **Complete the following sentence by selecting the appropriate option.**

A member's continuing duty to maintain professional knowledge and skill so that a client or employer receives competent professional service forms part of the fundamental principle of:

▼

Picklist

integrity

professional competence and due care

professional behaviour

(b) **Respond to the following statement by selecting the appropriate option.**

Within the conceptual framework of threats and safeguards, continuing professional development (CPD) requirements form one of the safeguards created by the profession.

True ☑

False ☐

Task 1.7

Jacob, an AAT member in practice, is conducting a second interview of an excellent candidate (also an AAT member) for a senior post in Jacob's firm. When discussing remuneration the potential employee states she will bring a copy of the database of clients from her old firm to introduce new clients to Jacob's firm. She also says she knows a lot of negative information about her old firm which Jacob could use to gain clients from them.

(a) **Answer the following task by selecting the appropriate option.**

In order to behave in an ethical manner in these circumstances, what is the most appropriate action for Jacob to take following the interview?

Because she shows business acumen, offer her the job. ☐

Because she has breached the fundamental principles of integrity and confidentiality, report her to the AAT. ☐

Because she lacks integrity, inform her that she will not be offered the job. ☑

BPP
LEARNING MEDIA

Frankie, an AAT member in practice, has been accused of bringing the profession into disrepute when marketing his professional services.

(b) **Complete the following sentence by selecting the appropriate option.**

This accusation is most likely to arise if Frankie:

states in an advertisement that he is a fully qualified member of the AAT. ☐

makes a disparaging reference in an advertisement to the work of Iqbal, an ACCA member. ☑

refers in an advertisement to the fact that some of his employees are only part-qualified. ☐

Jessica Murray is an AAT member who has worked for many years in Salim & Wright LLP, a practice that has all but one of its branches in the UK, with the other branch based overseas in Europe. She has now become a partner in the practice along with Tim Salim and Godfrey Wright, and Jessica wishes to change the practice's name to Salim, Wright & Murray International LLP.

(c) **Identify the element of the proposed name that could be considered to be misleading, by dragging it in the 'misleading element' box and dragging the rest of the name in the 'Reasonable name' box.**

Reasonable name	Misleading element

Drag and drop options:

Salim, Wright & Murray		International		LLP

(d) **Complete the following statement of how a member should apply safeguards against threats in any particular circumstance by selecting the appropriate word(s) to fill each gap in the sentence.**

In exercising professional judgement a member should consider what a reasonable and informed [▼], having knowledge of all relevant information, including the [▼] of the threat and the safeguards applied, would conclude to be [▼].

Picklist
third party
fellow professional
cost
significance
acceptable
unacceptable

Task 1.8

Vernon, a member in practice, performs bookkeeping services for both Yen Ltd and Piston Ltd. The two companies are in dispute about a series of purchases that Yen Ltd made from Piston Ltd.

(a) **Complete the following sentence by selecting the appropriate option.**

For Vernon this situation threatens both the fundamental principles of:

[▼]

Picklist

objectivity and confidentiality

integrity and professional behaviour

confidentiality and professional competence

BPP
LEARNING MEDIA

Niall is a member in business. His cousin Oonagh has recently been employed by an organisation with which Niall has regular business dealings. Oonagh's position means that she would be able to offer Niall preferential treatment in the awarding of major contracts.

(b) **Answer the following task by selecting the appropriate option.**

What should Niall do?

Seek legal advice. ☐

Advise Oonagh of relevant threats and safeguards that will protect Niall should he receive such an offer from Oonagh's organisation. ☑

Immediately inform higher levels of management. ☐

(c) **Complete the following sentence by selecting the appropriate option from the selection below.**

The requirement for an AAT member in practice to be independent of a client applies in relation to: [▼]

Picklist

all clients

assurance clients only

Quentin is an AAT member in practice with Topping LLP. He is engaged on an assurance assignment for Nickel plc when he receives news that his grandmother has left him a 1% shareholding in Nickel plc in her will.

(d) **Complete the following sentence by selecting the appropriate option from the selection below.**

This situation presents a [1] [SI ▼] and the best course of action would be [2] [▼]

Picklist [1]

familiarity threat

self-interest threat

Picklist [2]

to remove Quentin from the assurance engagement

to inform the audit

committee of Nickel plc

Helena is employed by Elaprop LLP and has been part of an assurance team for its client, Bowen plc, for three years. Helena has been approached by Bowen plc with an offer of a senior job in the company's finance team.

(e) **Complete the following sentence by selecting the appropriate option.**

This situation presents SI ▼

Picklist

an intimidation threat

a self-interest threat

Answer the following task by selecting the appropriate option.

Which TWO of the following safeguards should Elaprop LLP have in place?

A policy requiring Helena to notify the firm of such an offer. ☐

A policy preventing Helena from entering employment negotiations with an assurance client. ☐

A policy requiring Helena to resign from the firm once an offer of employment is recived from an assurance client. ☐

A policy requiring Helena's removal from the assurance engagement with Bowen plc. ☑

Section 2

Task 2.1

(a) **Identify whether the following business values are set out in the Nolan Principles or not by dragging the relevant items to each box.**

Business value set out in Nolan principles	Business values not set out in Nolan principles
A	T
	T
H	

Trust

Accountability

Transparency

Honesty

Trevor, an AAT member, has not complied with the AAT Code of Professional Ethics.

(b) **Complete the following sentence by selecting the appropriate option.**

Disciplinary action will be taken against Trevor [▼]

Picklist

immediately

if his employer notifies the AAT of the non-compliance

if his conduct reflects adversely on the reputation of the AAT

Task 2.2

Gregory, an AAT member, has just started his own accounting business. One of his first clients, Cassandra, has asked Gregory to keep custody of £200 in cash for one month, when it will need to be paid to HM Revenue and Customs in settlement of Cassandra's income tax liability.

(a) **Answer the following task by selecting the appropriate option.**

What should Gregory do?

Keep a note of the amount of money but hold it in his established bank account. ☐

Hold the money separately from his own money and that of his business. ☑

Inform Cassandra that he cannot hold the money as he is not regulated by the Financial Services Authority (FSA). ☐

William is an AAT member in practice who acts on behalf of an elderly client Jordan. Last month William issued an invoice for £5,000 to Jordan for 'safeguarding services', which just involved being sole signatory on Jordan's bank account for a period of one month. He has now transferred £7,000 to himself from Jordan's bank account in settlement of the invoice plus £2,000 'late fees'. Following a complaint from Jordan's son, the police are now investigating William for fraud.

(b) **Answer the following task by selecting the appropriate option.**

Which Fraud Act 2006 offence is it most likely that William has committed?

Fraud by false representation ☐

Fraud by abuse of position ☑

Fraud by failing to disclose information ☐

BPP LEARNING MEDIA

Task 2.3

Alessandro is an AAT member in practice employed by Sueka LLP. He has acquired some information about Polina Ltd in the course of acting for the company on an assurance engagement.

(a) Complete the following sentence by selecting the appropriate option.

The principle of confidentiality imposes an obligation on Alessandro to refrain from:

▼

Picklist

using the information to the advantage of Sueka LLP

disclosing the information within Sueka LLP

disclosing the information to anyone at all

Susan, an AAT member, owns and runs a small accountancy practice with seven employees. She has failed to notify the Information Commissioner of the practice's data processing operations.

(b) Respond to the following statement by selecting the appropriate option.

Susan has committed a criminal offence and may be fined if convicted.

True ✓

False ☐

Task 2.4

(a) Answer the following question by selecting the appropriate option.

In which circumstance are AAT members specifically advised to seek professional advice before disclosing confidential information?

Where there is a professional duty to disclose in the public interest and this is not prohibited by law. ✓

Where disclosure is required by law. ☐

Where disclosure is permitted by law and is authorised by the client or employer. ☐

Bill is an AAT member in practice as a sole practitioner. He suspects terrorist financing activities are taking place at his client Hover Ltd.

(b) Complete the following sentence by selecting the appropriate option.

Bill should disclose his suspicions concerning Hover Ltd to

▼

Picklist

the police

the board of Hover Ltd

the Serious Organised Crime Agency

Task 2.5

(a) **Complete the following sentence by selecting the appropriate option.**

Breach by a member in practice of the duty to exercise reasonable care and skill means the member may be liable to the client for [▼]

Picklist

breach of contract and professional negligence

fraud and professional negligence

fraud and breach of confidentiality

breach of contract and breach of confidentiality

Lionel, an AAT member in business, has been asked by his employer to undertake a major project for which Lionel currently does not have sufficient specific training or experience.

(b) **Complete the following sentence by selecting the appropriate option.**

Lionel may nonetheless undertake the project if he [▼]

Picklist

has adequate support

informs the employer that his performance will be lacking in expertise

Task 2.6

Patrick is a member in practice in the UK who acts as a principal in relation to his client, Pippa Ltd. To help Pippa Ltd's finance director in his preparation of the company's financial statements, Patrick has agreed to prepare a receivables ledger control account reconciliation.

(a) **Complete the following sentence by selecting the appropriate option.**

Ownership of the reconciliation when it is complete is [▼]

Picklist

Patrick's
Pippa Ltd's

(b) **Identify the three conditions that must exist for an AAT member in practice to have a right of lien over the documents of a sole trader client, by writing the relevant conditions in the appropriate box.**

	Right of lien exists
Condition 1	
Condition 2	
Condition 3	

The documents belong to the client.	The documents are in the member's possession, however this has come about.
The documents belong to a third party.	Works has been done by the member on the documents for which the fee has been paid.
The documents are in the member's possession by proper means.	Work has been done by the member on the documents for which the fee is outstanding.

Task 2.7

Zoe, an AAT member in practice in the UK works for a large firm of accountants. Zoe has a client which refuses to make disclosure of a known error in its taxation affairs, after having had notice of the error and a reasonable time to reflect.

(a) **Complete the following sentence by selecting the appropriate option.**

Zoe is obliged to report the client's refusal and the facts surrounding it to

▼

Picklist

HM Revenue and Customs (HMRC)

the Serious Organised Crime Agency (SOCA),

the Money Laundering Reporting Offer (MLRO)

(b) **Respond to the following statement by selecting the appropriate option.**

An act of attempting to conceal criminal properly is only reportable as a money laundering offence if it involves amounts of £500 or more.

True ☐

False ☑

(c) **Complete the following sentence by inserting the appropriate figure.**

The maximum period of imprisonment that can be imposed on a person found guilty of money laundering is [   ] years.

Task 2.8

Malcolm, an AAT member employed by Dreed plc, is facing significant pressure from his employer to intentionally mislead the company's internal auditors.

Complete the following sentence by selecting the appropriate option.

Malcolm's situation represents [1] [▼]

and his immediate response should be to implement the safeguard of [2] [▼]

Picklist [1]

an intimidation threat

a self-review threat

Picklist [2]

obtaining advice from the AAT

resigning from Dreed plc

BPP
LEARNING MEDIA

Task 2.9

(a) Complete the following sentence by selecting the appropriate option.

If an AAT member makes any disclosures which are likely to prejudice an investigation following a report to the relevant person concerning money laundering, the member

Picklist

has committed the criminal offence of tipping off

should consult the AAT Ethics Advice Line

may be liable to disciplinary action

Rohinder is an AAT member on an assurance engagement at Poster plc. During the course of the engagement he has become aware of client staff disguising the nature and source of certain funds which Rohinder believes derive from tax evasion.

(b) Complete the following sentence by selecting the appropriate option.

Rohinder must report his suspicions so as to avoid a charge of ⬚

Picklist

money laundering

failure to report

tipping off

Task 2.10

Dominic, an AAT member, has been employed for some years by Hill plc. He feels that his immediate manager Serena poses a threat to his ability to perform his duties with the appropriate degree of professional competence and due care, as she has deliberately concealed evidence of criminal acts. Dominic has not been able to reduce this threat sufficiently with relevant safeguards. He therefore wishes to make a protected disclosure to the board of Hill plc.

(a) Answer the following task by selecting the appropriate option.

What is Dominic's position as a whistle-blower in relation to the Public Interest Disclosure Act?

He will not be protected unless he discloses to a legal adviser. ☐

He will be protected provided he acts in good faith. ☑

He will not be protected as this is not a qualifying disclosure. ☐

(b) **Answer the following task by selecting the appropriate options.**

To which TWO of the following disclosures does the Public Interest Disclosure Act extend?

Professional negligence ☐

Endangerment of an individual's health and safety ☑

Environmental damage ☑

Breach of contract ☐

When reporting suspicion of money laundering, an AAT member in practice must make a 'required disclosure'.

(c) **Identify which items of information should be included in the disclosure and which should not be by dragging the appropriate items to each box.**

Included in disclosure	Not included in disclosure

The identify of the suspect (if known)

The whereabouts of the suspe (if known)

Information on which suspicio of money laundering is based

The nature of the laundered property (if known)

The whereabouts of the laundered property (if known)

The type of money laundering offence that has been committe

AAT PRACTICE ASSESSMENT 1
PROFESSIONAL ETHICS IN
ACCOUNTING AND FINANCE

ANSWERS

Section 1

Task 1.1

Complete the following sentences by selecting the appropriate option.

The behaviour of a member who is straightforward and honest in all professional and business relationships is following the fundamental principle of | integrity. |

The conceptual framework approach requires members to

| identify, evaluate and respond to threats to compliance with fundamental principles. |

Task 1.2

(a) **The accountancy profession is committed to which of the following objectives?**

An outlook which is essentially commercial, achieved by being business minded and free from regulatory pressure. ☐

Rendering services to acceptable standards of conduct and performance. ☐

Acknowledgement of duties to society as a whole in addition to duties to

the employer or client. ☑

(b) **In the UK, which part of the Financial Reporting Council has direct responsibility for reviewing the way in which the professional accountancy bodies regulate their members?**

The Accounting Standards Board (ASB) ☐

The Accountancy and Actuarial Discipline Board (AADB) ☐

The Professional Oversight Board (POB) ☑

(c) **A code of business ethics in an organisation should be designed to help an individual in the organisation:**

| make the right choice between alternative courses of action. |

Task 1.3

Sponsoring body of the AAT	Not a sponsoring body of the AAT
CIMA	ACCA
CIPFA	CAI
ICAEW	IFAC
ICAS	FRC

Task 1.4

(a) **The AAT Code of Professional Ethics is an example of civil law.**

True ☐

False ☑

(b) **Which of the following is a valid reason for an organisation to introduce an ethical code?**

To ensure that there is consistency of conduct by employees across the organisation. ☑

To impose criminal sanctions on employees who fail to comply with the ethical code. ☐

Task 1.5

(a) **According to the Basel Committee on Banking Supervision, the definition of operational risk is:**

The risk of direct or indirect loss resulting from inadequate or failed processes, people and systems.

BPP LEARNING MEDIA

Task 1.5 (continued)

(b) **Cecily, a member in practice, wishes to enter into a professional relationship with a client which will almost certainly last for at least two years. As part of her customer due diligence processes, which of the following actions must Cecily take?**

Notify the AAT of the relationship. ☐

Verify the nature and value of the client's assets. ☐

Verify the client's identity on the basis of documents, data or other reliable information. ☑

....

Task 1.6

(a) **A member's continuing duty to maintain professional knowledge and skill so that a client or employer receives competent professional service forms part of the fundamental principle of:**

professional competence and due care.

(b) **Within the conceptual framework of threats and safeguards, continuing professional development (CPD) requirements form one of the safeguards created by the profession.**

True ☑

False ☐

....

Task 1.7

(a) **In order to behave in an ethical manner in these circumstances, what is the most appropriate action for Jacob to take following the interview?**

Because she shows business acumen, offer her the job. ☐

Because she has breached the fundamental principles of integrity and confidentiality report her to the AAT. ☐

Because she lacks integrity, inform her that she will not be offered the job ☑

Task 1.7 (continued)

(b) **This accusation is most likely to arise if Frankie:**

states in an advertisement that he is a fully qualified member of the AAT. ☐

makes a disparaging reference in an advertisement to the work of Iqbal, an ACCA member. ☑

refers in an advertisement to the fact that some if his employees are only part-qualified. ☐

(c)

Reasonable name		Misleading element
Salem, Wright & Murray	LLP	International

(d) In exercising professional judgement a member should consider what a reasonable and informed ⟨third party⟩, having knowledge of all relevant information, including the ⟨significance⟩ of the threat and the safeguards applied, would conclude to be ⟨unacceptable⟩.

··

Task 1.8

(a) **For Vernon this situation threatens both the fundamental principles of:**

objectivity and confidentiality.

Task 1.8 (continued)

(b) What should Niall do?

Seek legal advice. ☐

Advise Oonagh of relevant threats and safeguards that will protect Niall should he receive such an offer from Oonagh's organisation. ☑

Immediately inform higher levels of management ☐

(c) The requirement for an AAT member in practice to be independent of a client applies in relation to: assurance clients only.

(d) This situation presents a self-interest threat and the best course of action would be to remove Quentin from the assurance engagement.

(e) Complete the following sentence by selecting the appropriate option from the dropdown menu.

This situation presents a a self-interest threat.

Which TWO of the following safeguards should Elaprop LLP have in place?

A policy requiring Helena to notify the firm of such an offer. ☑

A policy preventing Helena from entering employment negotiations with an assurance client. ☐

A policy requiring Helena to resign from the firm once an offer of employment is received from an assurance client. ☐

A policy requiring Helena's removal from the assurance engagement with Bowen plc. ☑

Section 2

Task 2.1

(a) **Identify whether the following business values are set out in the Nolan Principles or not by dragging the relevant items to each box.**

Business values set out in Nolan principles	Business values not set out in Nolan principles
Accountability	Trust
Honesty	Transparency

(b) **Complete the following sentence by selecting the appropriate option.**

Disciplinary action will be taken against Trevor

if his conduct reflects adversely on the reputation of the AAT.

Task 2.2

(a) **Answer the following task by selecting the appropriate option.**

What should Gregory do?

Keep a note of the amount of money but hold it in his established bank account.

Hold the money separately from his own money and that of his business. ✓

Inform Cassandra that he cannot hold the money as he is not regulated by the Financial Services Authority (FSA).

BPP
LEARNING MEDIA

Task 2.2 (continued)

(b) **Answer the following task by selecting the appropriate option.**

Which Fraud Act 2006 offence is it most likely that William has committed?

Fraud by false representation ☐

Fraud by abuse of position ☑

Fraud by failing to disclose information ☐

Task 2.3

(a) **Complete the following sentence by selecting the appropriate option.**

The principle of confidentiality imposes an obligation on Alessandro to refrain from:

> using the information to the advantage of Sueka LLP.

(b) **Respond to the following statement by selecting the appropriate option.**

Susan has committed a criminal offence and may be fined if convicted.

True ☑

False ☐

Task 2.4

(a) **Answer the following task by selecting the appropriate option.**

In which circumstance are AAT members specifically advised to seek professional advice before disclosing confidential information?

Where there is a professional duty to disclose in the public interest and this is not prohibited by law. ☑

Where disclosure is required by law. ☐

Where disclosure is permitted by law and is authorised by the client or employer. ☐

Task 2.4 (continued)

(b) **Complete the following sentence by selecting the appropriate option.**

Bill should disclose his suspicions concerning Hover Ltd to
the Serious Organised Crime Agency.

Task 2.5

(a) **Complete the following sentence by selecting the appropriate option.**

Breach by a member in practice of the duty to exercise reasonable care and skill means the member may be liable to the client for
breach of contract and professional negligence.

(b) **Complete the following sentence by selecting the appropriate option.**

Lionel may nonetheless undertake the project if he has adequate support.

Task 2.6

(a) **Complete the following sentence by selecting the appropriate option.**

Ownership of the reconciliation when it is complete is Pippa Ltd's.

BPP
LEARNING MEDIA

Task 2.6 (continued)

(b) **Identify the three conditions that must exist for an AAT member in practice to have a right of lien over the documents of a sole trader client, by writing the relevant conditions in the appropriate box.**

	Right of lien exists	
Condition 1	The documents are in the member's possession by proper means.	
Condition 2	The documents belong to the client.	
Condition 3	Work has been done by the member on the documents for which the fee is outstanding.	

The documents are in the member's possession, however this has come about.

The documents belong to a third party.

Works has been done by the member on the documents for which the fee has been paid.

Task 2.7

(a) **Complete the following sentence by selecting the appropriate option.**

Zoe is obliged to report the client's refusal and the facts surrounding it to the Money Laundering Reporting Officer (MLRO).

(b) **Respond to the following statement by selecting the appropriate option.**

An act of attempting to conceal criminal properly is only reportable as a money laundering offence if it involves amounts of £500 or more.

True ☐

False ☑

Task 2.7 (continued)

(c) **Complete the following sentence by inserting the appropriate figure.**

The maximum period of imprisonment that can be imposed on a person found guilty of money laundering is 14 years.

Task 2.8

Complete the following sentence by selecting the appropriate option.

Malcolm's situation represents an intimidation threat and his immediate

response should be to implement the safeguard of obtaining advice from the AAT.

Task 2.9

(a) **Complete the following sentence by selecting the appropriate option.**

If an AAT member makes any disclosures which are likely to prejudice an investigation following a report to the relevant person concerning money laundering, the member has committed the criminal offence of tipping off.

(b) **Complete the following sentence by selecting the appropriate option.**

Rohinder must report his suspicions so as to avoid a charge of failure to report.

Task 2.10

(a) **Answer the following task by selecting the appropriate option.**

What is Dominic's position as a whistle-blower in relation to the Public Interest Disclosure Act?

He will not be protected unless he discloses to a legal adviser. ☐

He will be protected provided he acts in good faith. ☑

He will not be protected as this is not a qualifying disclosure. ☐

Task 2.10 (continued)

(b) **Answer the following task by selecting the appropriate options.**

To which TWO of the following disclosures does the Public Interest Disclosure Act extend?

Professional negligence

Endangerment of an individual's health and safety ✓

Environmental damage ✓

Breach of contract

(c) **Identify which items of information should be included in the disclosure and which should not be by drawing a line between the appropriate items and the relevant box.**

Included in disclosure	Not included in disclosure
The identify of the suspect (if known)	The whereabouts of the suspect (if known)
Information on which suspicion of money laundering is based	The nature of the laundered property (if known)
The whereabouts of the laundered property (if known)	The type of money laundering offence that has been committed

AAT PRACTICE ASSESSMENT 2
PROFESSIONAL ETHICS IN
ACCOUNTING AND FINANCE

Time allowed: 1 hour 30 minutes

AAT PRACTICE
ASSESSMENT 2

The AAT assessment has been updated for the guidance expected to apply to assessments from 1 September 2012.

Section 1

Task 1.1

Complete the following sentences about the AAT's code of fundamental principles by selecting the appropriate option.

'A member who does not allow bias or undue influence of others to override professional or business judgements is following the fundamental principle of [▼]

Picklist
objectivity
professional competence and due care
integrity

'The conceptual framework approach requires members to apply adequate safeguards to eliminate or reduce threats to [▼]

Picklist
compliance with the fundamental principles
compliance with the law

Task 1.2

(a) **Identify whether each of the following statements is true or false by selecting the appropriate option.**

Statement	True	False
The AAT Code of Professional Ethics is a set of legal rules governing members of AAT.	☐	☐
The AAT Code of Professional Ethics applies to all members of AAT but only when they are acting for reward.	☐	☐

Task 1.2 (continued)

AAT members in business work in a huge variety of industries. Certain forms of regulation affect all members in business while other forms affect only those working in specific industries.

(b) **Select the appropriate option in each case to identify whether ALL members in business are affected by the following forms of regulation.**

Form of regulation	All AAT members in business affected	Not all AAT members in business affected
Health and safety laws	☐	☐
Code of practice for the financial services industry	☐	☐
Employment protection laws	☐	☐

Task 1.3

(a) **Answer the following task by selecting the appropriate option.**

Which of the following bodies sponsors the AAT?

Association of Chartered Certified Accountants (ACCA) ☐

International Federation of Accountants (IFAC) ☐

Financial Reporting Council (FRC) ☐

Chartered Institute of Management Accountants (CIMA) ☐

(b) **Identity whether the following statement is true or false by selecting the appropriate option.**

The AAT Code of Professional Ethics is based on the Code of Ethics for Professional Accountants approved by the International Federation of Accountants (IFAC).

True ☐

False ☐

BPP LEARNING MEDIA

Task 1.4

Complete the following sentences by selecting the appropriate option.

One of the Institute of Business Ethics' (IBE) simple ethical tests for a business decision is related to transparency. When considering transparency, the employee will ask himself or herself:

▼

Picklist

Who does my decision affect or hurt?

Do I mind others knowing what I have decided?

Would my decision be considered fair by those affected?

'If a code of ethics conflicts with legally enforceable rules, | ▼ |

Picklist

the legal rules must be followed'

the code of ethics must be followed'

Task 1.5

Rodrigo, a member in practice as a sole practitioner, occupies business premises in an area where severe floods are common.

(a) **Answer the following question by selecting the appropriate option.**

What type of operational risk is Rodrigo facing?

Political risk   ☐

Physical risk   ☐

Social risk   ☐

(b) **Complete the following sentence by selecting the appropriate option.**

'Where the Money Laundering Regulations apply to a new client relationship but it is not possible to complete adequate customer due diligence, a member in practice must…

…decline to enter into the client relationship.'   ☐

…enter into the client relationship with a suitably worded letter of engagement.'   ☐

Task 1.6

(a) **Complete the following sentence by selecting the most appropriate option.**

'The fundamental principle of professional competence and due care requires that a member must…

…undertake continuing professional development (CPD).' ☐

…maintain an adequate level of professional indemnity insurance.' ☐

…complete a set of AAT assessments every year.' ☐

(b) **Complete the following sentence by selecting the most appropriate option.**

'The AAT's CPD Cycle comprises four steps: assess, plan, action and

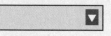

Picklist

evaluate'

develop'

Task 1.7

Annabelle, an AAT member in an accountancy firm, has recently recruited Leonard, an AAT student member, to the firm. She has noticed that Leonard frequently uses the firm's phone for personal international calls, and his workstation's computer to spend time on social networking sites.

(a) **Answer the following task by selecting the appropriate option.**

In order to behave in a sensitive manner in these circumstances, what is the most appropriate action for Annabelle to take immediately?

Discuss Leonard's behaviour with everyone in the office as soon as he is absent. ☐

Discuss his behaviour with Leonard and encourage him to change it. ☐

Inform her line manager and demand that Leonard be dismissed. ☐

Task 1.7 (continued)

Rebecca is a member in practice who has been approached by Gordon, her brother, to act for Jennings Ltd. Gordon is the Finance Director of Jennings Ltd.

(b) **Complete the following sentence by selecting the appropriate option.**

'Before accepting this new client relationship with Jennings Ltd Rebecca should consider whether acceptance would create any threats to compliance with the fundamental principles of...

...integrity, and professional competence and due care.' ☐

...objectivity, and professional behaviour.' ☐

...confidentiality, and professional competence and due care.' ☐

Raoul is a member in practice. Raoul's firm, Manson LLP, has been asked to give a quote for performing some work for a potential new client Manson LLP has quoted a fee that is so low that Raoul believes it may be difficult to perform the engagement in accordance with applicable technical and professional standards for that fee.

(c) **Identity how the situation represents a threat to a fundamental principle by selecting the appropriate option.**

This is a self-interest threat to professional behaviour. ☐

This is an advocacy threat to professional behaviour. ☐

This is a self-interest threat to professional competence and due care. ☐

This is an advocacy threat to professional competence and due care. ☐

Otto is an AAT member employed by Tillings plc, a manufacturer. Tillings plc has suffered a large reduction in business in the last year and Otto is now aware that his continued employment by the company is in doubt.

(d) **Complete the following sentence by identifying the most appropriate option.**

'The circumstances indicate that Otto may face...

...a self-review threat to the fundamental principles.' ☐

...a self-interest threat to the fundamental principles.' ☐

...an advocacy threat to the fundamental principles.' ☐

...a familiarity threat to the fundamental principles.' ☐

Task 1.8

William is a member in practice as a sole practitioner who has acted for many years for Grierson Ltd. William has now been asked to undertake an engagement by Figes Ltd, which is Grierson Ltd's greatest competitor. William has the ability to undertake the engagement and would like to do so, but realises that he is facing a conflict of interest.

(a) **Answer the following task by selecting the appropriate option.**

Which of the following safeguards should William implement?

Act only for Grierson Ltd as the relationship is already established. ☐

Cease to act for Grierson Ltd and inform Figes Ltd that he cannot undertake the engagement. ☐

Take particular care in continuing to act for Grierson Ltd and undertaking the engagement for Figes Ltd. ☐

Obtain the consent of Grierson Ltd and Figes Ltd to him acting on matters where their respective interests are in conflict. ☐

Andrew is a member in practice. His client Forfar Ltd manufactures and markets giftware via a catalogue. At Christmas, Forfar Ltd's Finance Director offers Andrew and all the company's other suppliers a gift from its catalogue to the value of £20.

(b) **Answer the following question by selecting the appropriate option.**

May Andrew accept the gift?

No – a member in practice may never accept a gift from a client. ☐

No – a member in practice may not accept such a large gift. ☐

Yes – the offer is made in the normal course of business to Andrew and all other suppliers. ☐

Yes – at Christmas members in practice are entitled to receive gifts from clients. ☐

BPP
LEARNING MEDIA

Task 1.8 (continued)

Liam is a member in practice who has a close personal relationship with Diane, the Finance Director of a client.

(c) **Complete the following sentence by selecting the appropriate option.**

'In light of this personal relationship Liam faces...

...an advocacy threat to his objectivity.' ☐

...a familiarity threat to his objectivity.' ☐

...a familiarity threat to his professional conduct and due care.' ☐

A member in practice on an assurance engagement must be independent.

(d) **Complete the following sentence by selecting the appropriate option.**

'Independence in these circumstances means [▼]

Picklist

independence of mind only'

independence in appearance only'

independence of mind and in appearance'

Section 2

Task 2.1

(a) **Complete the following sentence by selecting the appropriate option.**

'A business's code of practice states that a business cheque for more than £50 must be signed by two different employees. This part of the code is designed to

▼

Picklist

speed up cheque processing

reduce the risk of fraud

make sure that blame is apportioned'

Anya is a full member of the AAT. She is being investigated for misconduct.

(b) **Identify whether each of the following circumstances is conclusive proof of Anya's misconduct under the AAT's Disciplinary Regulations by selecting the appropriate option.**

Circumstance	Conclusive proof of misconduct	Not conclusive proof of misconduct
Anya has failed to inform the AAT that she has been declared bankrupt.	☐	☐
Anya failed to reply to correspondence from the AAT on one occasion.	☐	☐

Task 2.2

Frank is an AAT member in practice who has performed adequate due diligence on all his clients. He maintains a separate bank account for clients' monies and accounts for all monies properly. He provides investment business services to one client. Frank has never registered with the Financial Services Authority (FSA).

(a) **Answer the following question by selecting the appropriate option.**

With which set of procedures has Frank failed to comply?

Anti-money laundering procedures ☐

Anti-fraud procedures ☐

Investment business procedures ☐

BPP
LEARNING MEDIA

Task 2.2 (continued)

(b) **Identify whether each of the following statements is true or false by selecting the appropriate option.**

Statement	True	False
Conviction of a Fraud Act 2006 offence will give an AAT member a criminal record.	☐	☐
Breach of the AAT Code for handling clients' monies will give an AAT member in practice a criminal record.	☐	☐

Task 2.3

Martha, an AAT member in business, has recently started a new job with her previous employer's biggest competitor.

(a) **Complete each of the following sentences by selecting the appropriate option.**

'In her new job, Martha [▼] entitled to use the prior experience that she gained with her previous employer.'

Picklist

is

is not

'In her new job, Martha [▼] use confidential information acquired from her previous job.'

Picklist

may

may not

(b) **Identify whether the following statement is true or false by selecting the appropriate option.**

'Where information is obtained in circumstances that give rise to a duty of confidentiality, the AAT member has a legal obligation as well as an ethical obligation to maintain its confidentiality.'

True ☐

False ☐

Task 2.4

Lenny, an AAT member in practice, possesses some information about a client, Ormitron Ltd, which he knows he is legally obliged to keep confidential. Lenny is also aware that the AAT Code of Professional Ethics identifies circumstances when disclosure of the information may be appropriate.

(a) **Identify whether disclosure by Lenny may be appropriate in each of the following circumstances by selecting the relevant option.**

Circumstance	May be appropriate to disclose	Not appropriate to disclose
Disclosure is permitted by law but has not been authorised by Ormitron Ltd.	☐	☐
Disclosure is required as evidence in the course of legal proceedings involving Ormitron Ltd.	☐	☐

(b) **Complete the following sentence by selecting the appropriate option.**

'Where there is a professional duty to disclose confidential information, a member is only required to make disclosure if [▼]

Picklist

disclosure is not in the public interest'

disclosure is not prohibited by law'

disclosure is both in the public interest and not prohibited by law'

Task 2.5

(a) **Complete the following sentence by selecting the appropriate option.**

'Working outside the limits of his or her own professional experience, knowledge and expertise is a threat to an AAT member's compliance with the fundamental principle of [▼]

Picklist

confidentiality'

professional competence and due care'

objectivity'

BPP LEARNING MEDIA

Task 2.5 (continued)

Jacintha is an AAT member in business employed by Frantic Ltd. She has been asked to undertake a task for which she does not have sufficient specific training or experience, although she would like to do it. She is aware that the AAT Code of Professional Ethics requires her to take certain actions and prevent her from taking certain other actions in these circumstances.

(b) **Identify whether Jacintha must or must not take each of the following actions by selecting the appropriate option.**

Action	Must take	Must not take
Intentionally mislead Frantic Ltd as to her expertise and experience.	☐	☐
Seek appropriate expert advice and assistance.	☐	☐

Task 2.6

(a) **Complete the following statements by selecting the appropriate option.**

'Where an AAT member in practice acts as principal in relation to a client, documents created by the member on the specific instructions of the client belong to the

Picklist

client'
member'

'Where an AAT member acts as a client's agent any documents are generally the property of the [▼]

Picklist

client'
member'

'Where an AAT member in practice acts as principal in relation to a client, documents created by the member for the member's own purpose as a principal belong to the

[▼]

Picklist

client'
member'

George is an AAT member in practice in the UK who has obtained a court judgement for payment of a debt owed to him by a former client, Jade.

(b) **Complete the following statement by inserting the appropriate figure.**

'George must take action to enforce the judgement against Jade within [   ] years.'

Task 2.7

Merle is an AAT member in practice with a large firm of accountants. She suspects that the funds used by one of her clients arise from terrorist financing, but she has no evidence to support her suspicion.

(a) **Answer the following task by selecting the appropriate option.**

What should Merle do?

Take no action until she has obtained evidence to support her suspicion. ☐

Report her suspicion to the firm's Money Laundering Reporting Officer as the relevant authority. ☐

Report her suspicion to the Serious Organised Crime Agency as the relevant authority. ☐

(b) **Identify whether each of the following statements is true or false by selecting the appropriate option.**

Statement	True	False
An accountant who fails to disclose the concealment of criminal property may be accused of the criminal offence of money laundering.	☐	☐
Money laundering only needs to be reported to the relevant authority if it involves funds of more than £1,000.	☐	☐

Task 2.8

Marjot is an AAT member in business. He is facing pressure from his employer, Townsend Ltd, to lie to Townsend Ltd's industry regulator.

Answer the following task by selecting the appropriate option.

What should Marjot do first?

Notify the industry regulator. ☐

Contact the AAT Ethics Advice Line. ☐

Resign from Townsend Ltd. ☐

Task 2.9

Henry, an AAT member in practice as a sole practitioner in the UK, suspects that money he is holding on behalf of a client, Diane, is criminal property. As the money will soon be transferred to a non-UK bank account, he has decided to do nothing.

Complete the following sentence by selecting the appropriate option.

'Henry has committed the criminal offences of [▼]

Picklist

tipping off and failing to disclose'
failure to disclose and money laundering'
tipping off and money laundering'

'Henry should have made [▼] when he became aware of the matter.'

Picklist

an internal report
a suspicious activity report

'If he had made a report promptly Henry [▼]

Picklist

would still have committed both offences
would not have committed either offence

Task 2.10

Sandy, an AAT member in practice as a sole practitioner, suspects money laundering of property by his client Ishbel. Sandy is aware that the required disclosure he must submit to the relevant authority must detail Ishbel's identity and his reasons for suspicion.

(a) **Answer the following questions by identifying the appropriate option.**

What other fact must be contained in Sandy's required disclosure?

Where the laundered property is ☐

Where Ishbel is ☐

What the laundered property is ☐

In what type of report must Sandy submit his required disclosure?

An internal report ☐

A suspicious activity report (SAR) ☐

A financial report ☐

May Sandy seek consent from the relevant authority to carry on with the client relationship with Ishbel?

Yes ☐

No ☐

An AAT member employed in business who wishes to 'blow the whistle' on the activities of an employer is protected by the Public Interest Disclosure Act (PIDA).

(b) **Identify whether each of the following statements is true or false by selecting the appropriate option.**

Statement	True	False
Any disclosure to any entity is a 'protected disclosure' under PIDA if the employee reasonably believes that the information disclosed is true.	☐	☐
An employer is not allowed to dismiss an employee who makes a protected disclosure under PIDA.	☐	☐

AAT PRACTICE ASSESSMENT 2
PROFESSIONAL ETHICS IN
ACCOUNTING AND FINANCE

ANSWERS

Section 1

Task 1.1

Complete the following sentences about the AAT's code of fundamental principles by selecting the appropriate option.

'A member who does not allow bias or undue influence of others to override professional or business judgements is following the fundamental principle of objectivity.'

'The conceptual framework approach requires members to apply adequate safeguards to eliminate or reduce threats to compliance with the fundamental principles.'

···

Task 1.2

(a) **Identify whether each of the following statements is true or false by selecting the appropriate option.**

Statement	True	False
The AAT Code of Professional Ethics is a set of legal rules governing members of AAT.	☐	✓
The AAT Code of Professional Ethics applies to all members of AAT but only when they are acting for reward.	☐	✓

AAT members in business work in a huge variety of industries. Certain forms of regulation affect all members in business while other forms affect only those working in specific industries.

(b) **Select the appropriate option in each case to identify whether ALL members in business are affected by the following forms of regulation.**

Form of regulation	All AAT members in business affected	Not all AAT members in business affected
Health and safety laws	✓	☐
Code of practice for the financial services industry	☐	✓
Employment protection laws	✓	☐

···

Task 1.3

(a) **Answer the following task by selecting the appropriate option.**

Which of the following bodies sponsors the AAT?

Association of Chartered Certified Accountants (ACCA) ☐

International Federation of Accountants (IFAC) ☐

Financial Reporting Council (FRC) ☐

Chartered Institute of Management Accountants (CIMA) ☑

(b) **Identity whether the following statement is true or false by selecting the appropriate option.**

The AAT Code of Professional Ethics is based on the Code of Ethics for Professional Accountants approved by the International Federation of Accountants (IFAC).

True ☑

False ☐

Task 1.4

Complete the following sentences by selecting the appropriate option.

One of the Institute of Business Ethics (IBE) ethical simple ethical tests for a business decision is related to transparency. When considering transparency, the employee will ask himself or herself: Do I mind others knowing what I have decided?

'If a code of ethics conflicts with legally enforceable rules, the legal rules must be followed.'

Task 1.5

Rodrigo, a member in practice as a sole practitioner, occupies business premises in an area where severe floods are common.

(a) **Answer the following Task by selecting the appropriate option.**

What type of operational risk is Rodrigo facing?

Political risk	☐
Physical risk	☑
Social risk	☐

(b) **Complete the following sentence by selecting the appropriate option.**

'Where the Money Laundering Regulations apply to a new client relationship but it is not possible to complete adequate customer due diligence, a member in practice must…

…decline to enter into the client relationship.'	☑
…enter into the client relationship with a suitably worded letter of engagement'	☐

··

Task 1.6

(a) **Complete the following sentence by selecting the most appropriate option.**

'The fundamental principle of professional competence and due care requires that a member must…

…undertake continuing professional development (CPD).'	☑
…maintain an adequate level of professional indemnity insurance.'	☐
…complete a set of AAT assessments every year.'	☐

(b) **Complete the following sentence by selecting the most appropriate option.**

'The AAT's CPD Cycle comprises four steps: assess, plan, action and

evaluate.'

··

Task 1.7

(a) **Answer the following task by selecting the appropriate option.**

In order to behave in a sensitive manner in these circumstances, what is the most appropriate action for Annabelle to take immediately?

Discuss Leonard's behaviour with everyone in the office as soon as he is absent. ☐

Discuss his behaviour with Leonard and encourage him to change it. ☑

Inform her line manager and demand that Leonard be dismissed. ☐

Rebecca is a member in practice who has been approached by Gordon, her brother, to act for Jennings Ltd. Gordon is the Finance Director of Jennings Ltd.

(b) **Complete the following sentence by selecting the appropriate option.**

'Before accepting this new client relationship with Jennings Ltd Rebecca should consider whether acceptance would create any threats to compliance with the fundamental principles of...

...integrity, and professional competence and due care.' ☐

...objectivity, and professional behaviour.' ☑

...confidentiality, and professional competence and due care.' ☐

Raoul is a member in practice. Raoul's firm, Manson LLP, has been asked to give a quote for performing some work for a potential new client Manson LLP has quoted a fee that is so low that Raoul believes it may be difficult to perform the engagement in accordance with applicable technical and professional standards for that fee.

(c) **Identity how the situation represents a threat to a fundamental principle by selecting the appropriate option.**

This is a self-interest threat to professional behaviour. ☐

This is an advocacy threat to professional behaviour. ☐

This is a self-interest threat to professional competence and due care. ☑

This is an advocacy threat to professional competence and due care. ☐

BPP
LEARNING MEDIA

Task 1.7 (continued)

Otto is an AAT member employed by Tillings plc, a manufacturer. Tillings plc has suffered a large reduction in business in the last year and Otto is now aware that his continued employment by the company is in doubt.

(d) **Complete the following sentence by identifying the most appropriate option.**

'The circumstances indicate that Otto may face...

...a self-review threat to the fundamental principles.' ☐

...a self-interest threat to the fundamental principles.' ☑

...an advocacy threat to the fundamental principles.' ☐

...a familiarity threat to the fundamental principles.' ☐

Task 1.8

William is a member in practice as a sole practitioner who has acted for many years for Grierson Ltd. William has now been asked to undertake an engagement by Figes Ltd, which is Grierson Ltd's greatest competitor. William has the ability to undertake the engagement and would like to do so, but realises that he is facing a conflict of interest.

(a) **Answer the following task by selecting the appropriate option.**

Which of the following safeguards should William implement?

Act only for Grierson Ltd as the relationship is already established. ☐

Cease to act for Grierson Ltd and inform Figes Ltd that he cannot undertake the engagement. ☐

Take particular care in continuing to act for Grierson Ltd and undertaking the engagement for Figes Ltd. ☐

Obtain the consent of Grierson Ltd and Figes Ltd to him acting on matters where their respective interests are in conflict. ☑

Task 1.8 (continued)

Andrew is a member in practice. His client Forfar Ltd manufactures and markets giftware via a catalogue. At Christmas, Forfar Ltd's Finance Director offers Andrew and all the company's other suppliers a gift from its catalogue to the value of £20.

(b) **Answer the following task by selecting the appropriate option.**

May Andrew accept the gift?

No – a member in practice may never accept a gift from a client. ☐

No – a member in practice may not accept such a large gift. ☐

Yes – the offer is made in the normal course of business to Andrew and all other suppliers. ☑

Yes – at Christmas members in practice are entitled to receive gifts from clients. ☐

Liam is a member in practice who has a close personal relationship with Diane, the Finance Director of a client.

(c) **Complete the following sentence by selecting the appropriate option.**

'In light of this personal relationship Liam faces...

...an advocacy threat to his objectivity.' ☐

...a familiarity threat to his objectivity.' ☑

...a familiarity threat to his professional conduct and due care.' ☐

A member in practice on an assurance engagement must be independent.

(d) **Complete the following sentence by selecting the appropriate option.**

'Independence in these circumstances means
independence of mind and in appearance.'

Section 2

Task 2.1

(a) **Complete the following sentence by selecting the appropriate option.**

'A business's code of practice states that a business cheque for more than £50 must be signed by two different employees. This part of the code is designed to

| reduce the risk of fraud.' |

Anya is a full member of the AAT. She is being investigated for misconduct.

(b) **Identify whether each of the following circumstances is conclusive proof of Anya's misconduct under the AAT's Disciplinary Regulations by selecting the appropriate option.**

Circumstance	Conclusive proof of misconduct	Not conclusive proof of misconduct
Anya has failed to inform the AAT that she has been declared bankrupt.	✓	☐
Anya failed to reply to correspondence from the AAT on one occasion.	☐	✓

Task 2.2

Frank is an AAT member in practice who has performed adequate due diligence on all his clients. He maintains a separate bank account for clients' monies and accounts for all monies properly. He provides investment business services to one client. Frank has never registered with the Financial Services Authority (FSA).

(a) **Answer the following Task by selecting the appropriate option.**

With which set of procedures has Frank failed to comply?

Anti-money laundering procedures ☐

Anti-fraud procedures ☐

Investment business procedures ✓

Task 2.2 (continued)

(b) **Identify whether each of the following statements is true or false by selecting the appropriate option.**

Statement	True	False
Conviction of a Fraud Act 2006 offence will give an AAT member a criminal record.	✓	☐
Breach of the AAT Guidelines for handling clients' monies will give an AAT member in practice a criminal record.	☐	✓

Task 2.3

Martha, an AAT member in business, has recently started a new job with her previous employer's biggest competitor.

(a) **Complete each of the following sentences by selecting the appropriate option.**

'In her new job, Martha is entitled to use the prior experience that she gained with her previous employer.'

'In her new job, Martha may not use confidential information acquired from her previous job.'

(b) **Identify whether the following statement is true or false by selecting the appropriate option.**

'Where information is obtained in circumstances that give rise to a duty of confidentiality, the AAT member has a legal obligation as well as an ethical obligation to maintain its confidentiality.'

True ✓

False ☐

BPP
LEARNING MEDIA

Task 2.4

(a) **Identify whether disclosure by Lenny may be appropriate in each of the following circumstances by selecting the relevant option.**

Circumstance	May be appropriate to disclose	Not appropriate to disclose
Disclosure is permitted by law but has not been authorised by Ormitron Ltd.	☐	☑
Disclosure is required as evidence in the course of legal proceedings involving Ormitron Ltd.	☑	☐

(b) **Complete the following sentence by selecting the appropriate option.**

'Where there is a professional duty to disclose confidential information, a member is only required to make disclosure if

disclosure is both in the public interest and not prohibited by law.'

Task 2.5

(a) **Complete the following sentence by selecting the appropriate option.**

'Working outside the limits of his or her own professional experience, knowledge and expertise is a threat to an AAT member's compliance with the fundamental principle of

professional competence and due care.'

Jacintha is an AAT member in business employed by Frantic Ltd. She has been asked to undertake a task for which she does not have sufficient specific training or experience, although she would like to do it. She is aware that the AAT Code of Professional Ethics requires her to take certain actions and prevent her from taking certain other actions in these circumstances.

(b) **Identify whether Jacintha must or must not take each of the following actions by selecting the appropriate option.**

Action	Must take	Must not take
Intentionally mislead Frantic Ltd as to her expertise and experience.	☐	☑
Seek appropriate expert advice and assistance.	☑	☐

Task 2.6

(a) **Complete the following statements by selecting the appropriate option.**

'Where an AAT member in practice acts as principal in relation to a client, documents created by the member on the specific instructions of the client belong to the client.'

'Where an AAT member acts as a client's agent any documents are generally the property of the client.'

'Where an AAT member in practice acts as principal in relation to a client, documents created by the member for the member's own purpose as a principal belong to the member.'

George is an AAT member in practice in the UK who has obtained a court judgement for payment of a debt owed to him by a former client, Jade.

(b) **Complete the following statement by inserting the appropriate figure.**

George must take action to enforce the judgement against Jade within 12 years.'

Task 2.7

Merle is an AAT member in practice with a large firm of accountants. She suspects that the funds used by one of her clients arise from terrorist financing, but she has no evidence to support her suspicion.

(a) **Answer the following task by selecting the appropriate option.**

What should Merle do?

Take no action until she has obtained evidence to support her suspicion. ☐

Report her suspicion to the firm's Money Laundering Reporting Officer as the relevant authority. ☑

Report her suspicion to the Serious Organised Crime Agency as the relevant authority. ☐

BPP
LEARNING MEDIA

Task 2.7 (continued)

(b) **Identify whether each of the following statements is true or false by selecting the appropriate option.**

Statement	True	False
An accountant who fails to disclose the concealment of criminal property may be accused of the criminal offence of money laundering.	☐	✓
Money laundering only needs to be reported to the relevant authority if it involves funds of more than £1,000.	☐	✓

Task 2.8

Marjot is an AAT member in business. He is facing pressure from his employer, Townsend Ltd, to lie to Townsend Ltd's industry regulator.

Answer the following task by selecting the appropriate option.

What should Marjot do first?

Notify the industry regulator. ☐

Contact the AAT Ethics Advice Line. ✓

Resign from Townsend Ltd. ☐

Task 2.9

Henry, an AAT member in practice as a sole practitioner in the UK, suspects that money he is holding on behalf of a client, Diane, is criminal property. As the money will soon be transferred to a non-UK bank account, he has decided to do nothing.

Complete the following sentence by selecting the appropriate option.

'Henry has committed the criminal offences of failure to disclose and money laundering.'

'Henry should have made a suspicious activity report when he became aware of the matter.'

'If he had made a report promptly Henry would not have committed either offence.'

Task 2.10

Sandy, an AAT member in practice as a sole practitioner, suspects money laundering of property by his client Ishbel. Sandy is aware that the required disclosure he must submit to the relevant authority must detail Ishbel's identity and his reasons for suspicion.

(a) **Answer the following questions by identifying the appropriate option.**

What other fact must be contained in Sandy's required disclosure?

Where the laundered property is	☑
Where Ishbel is	☐
What the laundered property is	☐

In what type of report must Sandy submit his required disclosure?

An internal report	☐
A suspicious activity report (SAR)	☑
A financial report	☐

May Sandy seek consent from the relevant authority to carry on with the client relationship with Ishbel?

Yes	☑
No	☐

An AAT member employed in business who wishes to 'blow the whistle' on the activities of an employer is protected by the Public Interest Disclosure Act (PIDA).

(b) **Identify whether each of the following statements is true or false by selecting the appropriate option.**

Statement	True	False
Any disclosure to any entity is a 'protected disclosure' under PIDA if the employee reasonably believes that the information disclosed is true.	☐	☑
An employer is not allowed to dismiss an employee who makes a protected disclosure under PIDA.	☐	☑

BPP PRACTICE ASSESSMENT 1
PROFESSIONAL ETHICS IN
ACCOUNTING AND FINANCE

Time allowed: 1 hour 30 minutes

BPP
LEARNING MEDIA

PEAF BPP practice assessment 1

Section 1

Task 1.1

(a) **What is a key contributing factor to the effectiveness of an organisation's code of ethics?**

The willingness of employees to read it ☐

The corporate reputation of the organisation ☐

The level of management support 'from the top' ☐

(b) **Select the AAT's five fundamental principles of ethical behaviour from the picklist below.**

Fundamental Principle	
	▼
	▼
	▼
	▼
	▼

Picklist

Confidentiality
Accuracy
Professional behaviour
Courtesy
Professional competence and due care
Diligence
Integrity
Objectivity

Task 1.2

(a) **What is the final stage of the AAT's Disciplinary Process?**

The Disciplinary Tribunal ☐

Decisions and recommendations on grounds for action ☐

Member's response ☐

(b) **The AAT Code of Professional Ethics deals with inducements. Accepting significant inducements can give rise to self-interest and intimidation threats to:**

Integrity and professional behaviour ☐

Objectivity and confidentiality ☐

Professional competence and due care and objectivity ☐

(c) **Which of the following should AAT members turn to if they have an ethical dilemma and are in any doubt as to the correct course of action?**

The Financial Reporting Council ☐

The AAT Ethics Advice Line ☐

The Serious Organised Crime Agency ☐

Task 1.3

(a) **Any commission paid to an AAT member for introducing a client to another firm has to be:**

Declared to the AAT ☐

Kept in a client money account ☐

Paid to the client unless the client agrees that the AAT member can keep it ☐

(b) **Which TWO of the following circumstances prevent an AAT member from holding a client's money?**

The money is suspected criminal property. ☐

The money exceeds £25,000. ☐

The money is from an investment business client. ☐

An appropriate level of interest cannot be earned from holding the money. ☐

(c) **Attempting to conceal criminal property is reportable as a money laundering offence regardless of the sums involved.**

True ☐

False ☐

Task 1.4

(a) Melanie, an AAT member in practice, suspects that one of her clients is engaged in deliberate tax evasion. Despite her best attempts to persuade them to undertake full and accurate disclosure of their affairs, they continue to evade their responsibilities.

What can Melanie do?

Resign from involvement in the client's tax affairs ☐

Report the situation to the tax authorities ☐

Report the situation to her firm's Money Laundering Reporting Officer ☐

(b) Sasha, an AAT member in practice, has just taken on a new client, and is about to commence fee negotiations for a piece of financial reporting work that she has been asked to undertake.

How can she make sure that she follows an ethical remuneration policy?

Agree the basis of the fee in advance with the client ☐

Propose that the fee be based upon the results of the financial reporting exercise ☐

Tell the client that she will let them know the fee at the end of the assignment, when all of her costs are known ☐

(c) Paige Smith is an AAT member in practice who has been working as a manager on an assurance engagement for a car dealership. At the end of the engagement, the Finance Director at the client offers Paige and the rest of the assurance team a significant amount off the purchase price of a new car.

What action should Paige take in respect of this offer?

Report the Finance Director to her firm's Money Laundering Reporting Officer ☐

Inform those charged with governance at the client ☐

Accept the offer on the basis that it is probably offered to all client employees ☐

Kindly decline the offer from the Finance Director as it may threaten the ethical principle of objectivity ☐

Task 1.5

Which of the following is an 'event' listed by the Basel Committee which represents an operational risk for business?

Misleading reporting ☐

Damage to physical assets ☐

Professional misconduct ☐

Task 1.6

(a) **The taxpaying client bears ultimate responsibility for the accuracy of the data and computations in a tax return prepared by an adviser.**

True ☐

False ☐

(b) Rebecca is planning to draw money out of her client's account to pay for outstanding fees. Rebecca maintains that she is owed £10,000, but the client insists that it is less.

How much can Rebecca withdraw from the account?

None – Rebecca is never allowed to touch client money, unless for a strictly specified purpose ☐

£10,000 ☐

£2,000 as a reasonable part payment ☐

None – the client needs to agree the amount to be withdrawn ☐

Task 1.7

(a) The partners at Brightstar LLP have worked closely with a client, Sara Ltd, for many years. They are concerned that their objectivity may be compromised after all this time, and wonder what they should do for the best.

What is the most likely threat to the fundamental ethical principle of objectivity?

Self-review ☐

Familiarity ☐

Advocacy ☐

BPP
LEARNING MEDIA

... and what should be done about it?

Rotation of personnel involved with Sara Ltd ☐

Establishment of mechanisms to encourage 'whistle-blowing' of staff concerns ☐

Quality control measures ☐

(b) Nick, an AAT member in practice, has let slip to one of his AAT student friends that his client company is in financial difficulties. He has done this to illustrate to his friend the problems that can arise when cash controls are poor. The friend in question has some shares in the client company, and is now intending to sell them.

What is the main fundamental ethical principle that Nick has violated?

Professional competence and due care ☐

Confidentiality ☐

Professional behaviour ☐

Task 1.8

(a) Janice, an AAT member, is being pressured by her manager to perform a task for which she feels she does not have the appropriate level of knowledge or experience. She has told him of her concerns, but he refuses to get her any additional help or support.

What should she do?

Report her manager to the AAT as an intimidation threat ☐

Ask for help from a friend in another accountancy firm who has done similar work before ☐

Refuse to undertake the assignment ☐

(b) Janet, an AAT member, has been told that the future of her job depends upon the success of her company's latest product, which she knows has faults but which is being promoted widely with no mention of them. She is being asked to sell the product to her friends.

What type of threat to her professional integrity does this represent?

Self-interest ☐

Self-review ☐

Advocacy ☐

Section 2

Task 2.1

(a) **Which TWO of the following member bodies of the Consultative Committee of Accountancy Bodies are sponsoring bodies of the AAT?**

Chartered Accountants Ireland ☐

The Association of Chartered Certified Accountants (ACCA) ☐

The Institute of Chartered Accountants of Scotland (ICAS) ☐

The Chartered Institute of Public Finance and Accountancy (CIPFA) ☐

(b) **Failure by a commercial organisation to prevent bribery is an offence under the Bribery Act 2010.**

True ☐

False ☐

Task 2.2

(a) Fiona, an AAT member offering taxation services, has told her clients that her relatively high fees are because she can promise results: her tax returns and advice have never been challenged by the taxation authorities.

Is this an ethical approach?

Yes – she has a history of good results and she can prove her expertise ☐

No – tax returns and advice are always open to challenge ☐

(b) A property developer who is a client of Fay, an AAT member, has written asking whether she knows of any businesses in the city looking to sell a commercial property.

She recalls that a cinema client has told her that they are intending to sell. However, she is also aware that the value of the property will fall, once a scheme for a new entertainment complex nearby is approved. Fay knows that she cannot disclose these facts, because they are both protected by:

Client confidentiality ☐

Public Interest Disclosure Act 1998 ☐

AAT Disciplinary Regulations ☐

Task 2.3

(a) **If an AAT member prepares financial statements covering up payroll fraud, he or she is party to the concealment of 'criminal property'.**

True ☐

False ☐

(b) A client has asked you to hold a significant amount of money on his behalf, pending the highly probable purchase by your client of another business.

Would you accept this money and if so how would you deal with it?

No; the amount is likely to be too large ☐

No; you need to verify the purchase first ☐

Yes; it must be held in a separate bank account ☐

(c) **Individuals found guilty of the offence of bribery under the Bribery Act 2010 face a maximum prison sentence of 14 years.**

True ☐

False ☐

Task 2.4

(a) **Which of the options below represents an example of a self-review threat?**

Financial incentives based upon results or profits ☐

Being asked to justify a decision that you have been involved in ☐

Commercial pressure ☐

(b) **Lia holds a significant number of shares in one of her firm's audit clients. The requirement to disclose these holdings, and any share trading, to the officials in charge of corporate governance in her organisation is an example of a safeguard against what kind of threat?**

Self-interest ☐

Self-review ☐

Intimidation ☐

Task 2.5

(a) Behaving in an ethical manner involves acting with honesty, fairness and sensitivity.

Which of the following describes sensitivity?

Treating others equally ☐

Respecting another's right to confidentiality and privacy ☐

Being truthful and avoiding the temptation to mislead or deceive others ☐

(b) Amelia, an AAT member in practice, has been asked by a client to provide a second opinion on some work done by another firm. It appears that she will not have access to the same information that the other firm had.

Give an example of a safeguard that could counteract this threat:

Refuse to undertake the assignment ☐

Ask for additional help from others in her firm ☐

Get permission to make contact with the other firm and obtain the information ☐

(c) **When a client approaches a member in practice to perform financial reporting services, that member is bound to accept the appointment, as long as enquiries have been made of the previous adviser and there are no fees outstanding.**

True ☐

False ☐

Task 2.6

Who receives the interest earned by a balance in a client money account?

The firm holding the money ☐

The client ☐

The tax authorities ☐

BPP
LEARNING MEDIA

Task 2.7

(a) **What can large firms do to protect conflicting client interests?**

Keep client contact details confidential ☐

Build 'Chinese walls' of different staff teams ☐

Never take on clients who are in direct competition with each other ☐

(b) **Recruitment, selection, appraisal, promotion, training and reward systems are examples of safeguards established by the professional bodies against threats to ethical principles such as objectivity.**

True ☐

False ☐

Task 2.8

(a) **Jemima, an AAT member, has been found guilty of fraud under the Fraud Act 2006. What punishment might she expect?**

A prison sentence only ☐

A prison sentence or an unlimited fine ☐

Payment of damages ☐

(b) **Involvement in any investment activity by AAT members in the UK requires authorisation by the**

FRC ☐

FSA ☐

AAT ☐

(c) **Fill in the missing word below by selecting the appropriate option.**

Section 3 of the Fraud Act 2006 covers fraud by failing to [▼] information.

Picklist

detect
disclose
prepare

Task 2.9

(a) **Which industry sector is the Basel Committee most closely associated with?**

Insurance ☐

Banking ☐

Retail ☐

(b) **Which of the following bodies can fine or impose other sanctions on accountants whose work fails to meet professional standards?**

Accounting Standards Board (ASB) ☐

Accountancy and Actuarial Discipline Board (AADB) ☐

Financial Reporting Review Panel (FRRP) ☐

Task 2.10

(a) **The threat of disciplinary action can be an effective safeguard against threats to objectivity.**

True ☐
False ☐

(b) **How is the AAT Code of Professional Ethics related to the objectives of the accountancy profession?**

There is no particular relationship, because different bodies have drafted them. ☐

If an accountant understands the objectives, he or she will automatically be complying with the AAT Code of Professional Ethics. ☐

The AAT Code of Professional Ethics aims to assist members to achieve the objectives. ☐

BPP
LEARNING MEDIA

BPP PRACTICE ASSESSMENT 1
PROFESSIONAL ETHICS IN
ACCOUNTING AND FINANCE

ANSWERS

BPP
LEARNING MEDIA

PEAF BPP practice assessment 1

Section 1

Task 1.1

(a) The correct answer is: The level of management support 'from the top'

(b) The correct answer is:

Fundamental Principle
Integrity
Objectivity
Professional competence and due care
Confidentiality
Professional behaviour

Task 1.2

The correct answers are:

(a) The Disciplinary Tribunal

(b) Objectivity and confidentiality

(c) The AAT Ethics Advice Line

Task 1.3

(a) The correct answer is: Paid to the client unless the client agrees that the AAT member can keep it.

(b) The correct answers are:

- The money is suspected criminal property.

- The money is from an investment business client.

(c) The correct answer is: True

Task 1.4

The correct answers are:

(a)   Report the situation to her firm's Money Laundering Reporting Officer

(b)   Agree the basis of the fee in advance with the client

(c)   Kindly decline the offer as it may threaten the ethical principle of objectivity

Task 1.5

The correct answer is: Damage to physical assets

Task 1.6

(a)   The correct answer is: True

(b)   The correct answer is: None – the client needs to agree the amount to be withdrawn.

Monies should only be drawn from the client account on the client's instruction, or for the benefit of the client.

Task 1.7

The correct answers are:

(a)   • Familiarity

• Rotation of personnel involved with Sara Ltd

(b)   Confidentiality

Task 1.8

The correct answers are:

(a)   Refuse to undertake the assignment

(b)   Self-interest

BPP
LEARNING MEDIA

Section 2

Task 2.1

The correct answers are:

(a) • The Institute of Chartered Accountants of Scotland (ICAS)

   • The Chartered Institute of Public Finance and Accountancy (CIPFA)

(b) True

Task 2.2

The correct answers are:

(a) No – tax returns and advice are always open to challenge

(b) Client confidentiality

Task 2.3

The correct answers are:

(a) True

(b) Yes; it must be held in a separate bank account

(c) False; the maximum prison sentence for individuals found guilty of bribery under the Bribery Act 2010 is ten years.

Task 2.4

The correct answers are:

(a) Being asked to justify a decision that you have been involved in

(b) Self-interest

Task 2.5

The correct answers are:

(a) Respecting another's right to confidentiality and privacy

(b) Get permission to make contact with the other firm and obtain the information

(c) False.

Task 2.6

The correct answer is: The client

Task 2.7

The correct answers are:

(a) Build 'Chinese walls' of different staff teams.

(b) False – they are safeguards set up *in the workplace* rather than by the professional bodies themselves.

Task 2.8

The correct answers are:

(a) A prison sentence or an unlimited fine

(b) FSA

(c) Fraud by failing to | disclose | information

Task 2.9

The correct answers are:

(a) Banking

(b) Accountancy and Actuarial Discipline Board (AADB)

Task 2.10

The correct answers are:

(a) True

(b) The AAT Code of Professional Ethics aims to assist members to achieve the objectives.

BPP
LEARNING MEDIA

BPP PRACTICE ASSESSMENT 2
PROFESSIONAL ETHICS IN
ACCOUNTING AND FINANCE

Time allowed: 1 hour 30 minutes

BPP PRACTICE ASSESSMENT 2
PROFESSIONAL ETHICS IN
ACCOUNTING AND FINANCE

Time allowed: 1 hour 30 minutes

PEAF BPP practice assessment 2

Section 1

Task 1.1

Fill in the blank by selecting the appropriate option:

'The AAT Code of Professional Ethics note that: 'the [▼] you make in the everyday course of your professional lives can have real ethical implications.'

Picklist
Decisions
Contacts
Money

Task 1.2

(a) Fabio works for Clarity LLP, a firm recognised as having high ethical standards, with an ethics committee and dedicated ethics officer. He is filling out his timesheet for the week, but cannot remember how many hours he worked on an assignment for Ricotta Ltd. He decides instead to charge time to a general administrative code in accordance with his firm's policy.

He is then questioned by one of the partners as to why his non-assigned time seems so high for the week and is told to charge more time to a large client who, the partner says, 'will never notice – remember going forward that I do not like non-chargeable time from junior staff members like you'.

How would you characterise Fabio's initial filling out of his timesheet?

He behaved with integrity. ☐

He was foolish to think that his time should not be charged out. ☐

He behaved with objectivity. ☐

(b) **Fabio agrees to amend his timesheet. What type of threat to the fundamental ethical principles did the partner's words represent?**

Self-interest ☐

Familiarity ☐

Intimidation ☐

(c) **If Fabio is uncomfortable with this turn of events, what is he advised to do?**

Seek advice from his firm's ethics committee ☐

Complain about the partner to his department manager ☐

Resign from his position ☐

Task 1.3

(a) Gavin, an AAT member, has just established his own practice and wants to offer referral fees to third parties to help him to get some new clients. He is proposing a fee of £1,000 per client that is successfully referred.

What is Gavin's position with this policy?

It is acceptable as long as the referred client is aware of the fee and agrees to it being paid. ☐

It is unacceptable because it represents a threat to the objectivity of the third parties involved. ☐

£1,000 is too high a fee. ☐

(b) **Which of the following best illustrates the principle behind managing conflicts of interest?**

You can never take on clients with conflicting interests. ☐

The interests of one client must not have a negative effect on the interests of another. ☐

It is impossible to fully manage the interests of more than one client at a time. ☐

Task 1.4

Fill in the blanks by selecting the appropriate words from the picklist.

'A(n) [_____ ▼] financial interest is a financial interest beneficially owned through a collective investment vehicle, estate, [_____ ▼] or other intermediary over which the individual or entity has [_____ ▼] control.'

Picklist

trust

individual

indirect

no

full

direct

Task 1.5

(a) **As an AAT member in practice, what should you do if a statutory demand for information on one of your clients is made?**

Hand over all of the required information straightaway ☐

Seek legal advice ☐

Recommend that your client complies with the information request ☐

(b) Henry's client, George Ltd, is putting directors' private expenditure through its tax return as a business expense, in an attempt to reduce its tax liability.

What should Henry do?

Adjust the tax return to remove the private expenditure ☐

Explain his professional obligations – he cannot endorse a misleading tax return ☐

Ignore the private expenditure – his job is to get the best result for George Ltd ☐

Task 1.6

(a) **What are the main general principles governing how AAT members advertise their professional services?**

Effectiveness and integrity ☐

Integrity and professional behaviour ☐

Integrity and dignity ☐

(b) 'Holders of public office have a duty to declare any private interests relating to their public duties and to take steps to resolve any conflicts arising in a way that protects the public interest.'

Which of the Nolan Principles is being defined here?

Selflessness ☐

Openness ☐

Honesty ☐

(c) You have received a letter from a landlord, requesting financial information about one of your individual clients, who is applying to rent a property. The information is needed as soon as possible, by fax or e-mail, in order to secure approval for the client.

What ethical principle does this situation raise?

Professional competence and due care ☐

Confidentiality ☐

Professional behaviour ☐

Task 1.7

(a) **Ideally, how should minor ethical issues at work be resolved?**

Consultation with the AAT Ethics Advice Line ☐

Informal discussion with your immediate manager ☐

Consultation with the Accountancy and Actuarial Discipline Board ☐

(b) **What form of monitoring is the one largely adopted by the accountancy profession in the UK?**

Self-regulation ☐

Independent watchdog ☐

Government regulation ☐

(c) **Failure to comply with a professional code of practice can result in:**

Breach of contract and damages ☐

Professional negligence ☐

Expulsion from the relevant professional organisation ☐

(d) **If safeguards in the workplace are insufficient to counter a threat to one of the fundamental ethical principles, what should an AAT member do?**

Seek legal advice ☐

Refuse to act ☐

Report concerns to the AAT Director of Professional Development ☐

Task 1.8

(a) **Rowan, an AAT member in practice, has been offered a job by his client, Greene Ltd. What should he do as a first step, before considering the offer?**

Inform his manager that such an offer has been made ☐

Immediately resign from his current position ☐

Refuse the offer, as he is not allowed to accept it ☐

(b) Billy, an AAT member in practice, has just moved to expensive new offices in the centre of a major city. He enjoys the prestige associated with them, but is worried about the rental cost and proposes that he increase his charge-out rates to cover it.

Is this ethical?

Yes, it is acceptable to cover office overheads in charge-out rates. ☐

No, he chose to move to new offices and clients should not have to pay for them. ☐

Section 2

Task 2.1

(a) There is suspicion on the part of an AAT member that her client has supplied information for a tax return, recently prepared and submitted by the member, without checking the details.

Does the adviser have an ethical issue?

No – it is the client's responsibility as they have not checked the information. ☐

Yes – the adviser is in the position of supplying inaccurate or misleading information to HMRC. ☐

(b) **Disclosure of suspected money laundering is:**

A legal duty ☐

A professional duty ☐

Acceptable as long as confidentiality is respected ☐

Task 2.2

(a) Tom, an AAT member in practice, has just discovered that his friend has been offered a lucrative supply contract by a large company, which is a client of Tom's firm. Having prepared its financial statements, Tom is aware that the company is in serious financial difficulties – to the point that it may not be able to meet its financial obligations.

Can Tom disclose anything to his friend?

Yes – he has prepared the accounts which will soon be public knowledge anyway ☐

No – he cannot breach the confidentiality of his client ☐

(b) **What action could Tom take?**

Encourage his friend to accept a contract from another company that he knows is in better financial shape ☐

Encourage his friend to exercise due diligence before accepting any contract ☐

Report the client to the Financial Reporting Council for entering into contracts that it may not be able to honour ☐

BPP LEARNING MEDIA

(c) **What fundamental ethical principle must be balanced against the benefits of disclosure of matters in the public interest?**

Objectivity ☐

Integrity ☐

Confidentiality ☐

Task 2.3

(a) Ajay, an AAT member in practice, has been asked to prepare a bank reconciliation for a charity client of his firm. Ajay has never prepared a bank reconciliation for a charity before, but the accountant at the charity knows Ajay from her previous job and is happy to work with him.

What threat to his professional competence does this piece of work represent?

No threat – a bank reconciliation is not likely to be sector specific and Ajay should be equal to the task ☐

A threat – Ajay has never worked for a charity in this capacity before ☐

A threat – Ajay knows the accountant and this will affect his ability to perform the reconciliation properly ☐

(b) Charlie's main selling point for his new practice is his low fee rate. He currently has more clients than other practices of a similar size, and plans to recruit more staff. Last week he discovered an error in a tax return that he prepared recently.

What does this scenario illustrate?

If low fees are charged, you need to make sure that you can still offer a quality service. ☐

Low fees always mean a low quality service. ☐

Low fees always work well in attracting customers. ☐

What should Charlie do about the error in tax return?

Leave it until next year when he will have more staff ☐

Charge the client an extra fee to correct the error that he made ☐

Advise the client that the relevant tax authority must be notified of the error ☐

Task 2.4

Fill in the blanks in the following AAT definition of misconduct, using words from the picklist.

'[having] conducted him/herself in such a manner as would in the opinion of the

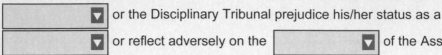

[⯆] or the Disciplinary Tribunal prejudice his/her status as a

[⯆] or reflect adversely on the [⯆] of the Association.'

Picklist
Investigations team
Member
Ethics
Serious Organised Crime Agency
Reputation
Professional

Task 2.5

(a) Stuart has been working for Pynn LLP for a year, since leaving Angus Ltd where he was an accountant in the marketing department. Angus Ltd has just appointed Pynn LLP to be its advisers and has asked the firm to undertake a financial reporting assignment.

   Should Stuart be involved on the assignment?

   No – there is a self-review threat here ☐

   Yes – as long as he abides by the fundamental ethical principles ☐

   No – he cannot be trusted to be objective ☐

(b) **Significant levels of unpaid fees from a client can constitute a threat to your objectivity and independence.**

   True ☐

   False ☐

BPP
LEARNING MEDIA

Task 2.6

(a) **Fill in the blank by selecting the appropriate option:**

Under UK law the ownership of working papers in respect to taxation services normally resides with [▼]

Picklist
The accountant
The client
HMRC

(b) 'All professional and business judgements should be made fairly.'

This statement is a definition of which ethical principle?

Integrity ☐

Objectivity ☐

Professional behaviour ☐

Task 2.7

(a) **Fill in the missing word below.**

Section 2 of the Fraud Act 2006 covers fraud by [   ] representation.

(b) **When advertising his or her practice, an AAT member must never make comparisons with competitors.**

True ☐

False ☐

Task 2.8

(a) **Fill in the blank by selecting the appropriate option:**

'[▼] risk is that arising from the carrying out of a company's business'

Picklist
Reputational
Strategic
Operational

(b) **Fill in the blank:**

Due care is a legal concept which states that, having accepted an assignment, you have [▼] to carry it out to the best of your ability.

Picklist

a contractual obligation
an ethical duty
a set amount of time

Task 2.9

Jenny, an AAT member in practice, has attended a seminar on ethics in the workplace. One of her colleagues made the statement: 'Ethics are black and white, and everyone needs to come to an agreement when an ethical issue arises at work.'

Is this statement correct?

Yes [ ]

No [ ]

Task 2.10

Which TWO of the following does the accountancy profession list as objectives?

The mastering of particular skills and techniques [ ]

Achieving the best possible outcomes for clients [ ]

Development of an ethical approach to work [ ]

Acknowledgement of duties to the financial services industry [ ]

BPP
LEARNING MEDIA

BPP PRACTICE ASSESSMENT 2
PROFESSIONAL ETHICS IN
ACCOUNTING AND FINANCE

ANSWERS

PEAF BPP practice assessment 2

Section 1

Task 1.1

The correct answer is: Decisions

....

Task 1.2

The correct answers are:

(a) He behaved with integrity

(b) Intimidation

(c) Seek advice from his firm's ethics committee

....

Task 1.3

The correct answers are:

(a) It is acceptable as long as the referred client is aware that the fee and agrees to it being paid

(b) The interests of one client must not have a negative effect on the interests of another.

....

Task 1.4

The correct answer is:

'An [indirect] financial interest is a financial interest beneficially owned through a collective investment vehicle, estate, [trust] or other intermediary over which the individual or entity has [no] control.'

....

Task 1.5

The correct answers are:

(a) Seek legal advice

(b) Explain his professional obligations – he cannot endorse a misleading tax return

---

Task 1.6

The correct answers are:

(a) Integrity and dignity

(b) Honesty

(c) Confidentiality

Task 1.7

The correct answers are:

(a) Informal discussion with your immediate manager

(b) Self-regulation

(c) Expulsion from the relevant professional organisation

(d) Refuse to act

Task 1.8

The correct answers are:

(a) Inform his manager that such an offer has been made

(b) Yes, it is acceptable to cover office overheads in charge-out rates

---

BPP
LEARNING MEDIA

Section 2

Task 2.1

The correct answers are:

(a) Yes – the adviser is in the position of supplying inaccurate or misleading information to HMRC

(b) A legal duty

Task 2.2

The correct answers are:

(a) No – he cannot breach the confidentiality of his client

(b) Encourage his friend to exercise due diligence before accepting any contract

(c) Confidentiality

Task 2.3

The correct answers are:

(a) No threat – a bank reconciliation is not likely to be sector specific and Ajay should be equal to the task

(b) • If low fees are charged, you need to make sure that you can still offer a quality service.

• Advise the client that the relevant tax authority must be notified of the error.

Task 2.4

The correct answers are:

'[having] conducted him/herself in such a manner as would in the opinion of the

Investigations Team or the Disciplinary Tribunal prejudice his/her status as a

member or reflect adversely on the reputation of the Association'.

Task 2.5

The correct answers are:

(a)   No – there is a self-review threat here

(b)   True

....

Task 2.6

The correct answers are:

(a)   The accountant

(b)   Objectivity

....

Task 2.7

The correct answers are:

(a)   Fraud by **false** representation

(b)   False

....

Task 2.8

The correct answers are:

(a)   Operational

(b)   A contractual obligation

....

Task 2.9

The correct answers is: No.

....

Task 2.10

The correct answers are:

- The mastering of particular skills and techniques
- Development of an ethical approach to work

....

BPP
LEARNING MEDIA

INDEX

BPP
LEARNING MEDIA

BPP LEARNING MEDIA

REVIEW FORM

How have you used this Combined Text and Question Bank?
(Tick one box only)

☐ Home study

☐ On a course_____

☐ Other _____

Why did you decide to purchase this Combined Text and Question Bank?
(Tick one box only)

☐ Have used BPP Texts in the past

☐ Recommendation by friend/colleague

☐ Recommendation by a college lecturer

☐ Saw advertising

☐ Other _____

During the past six months do you recall seeing/receiving either of the following?
(Tick as many boxes as are relevant)

☐ Our advertisement in Accounting Technician

☐ Our Publishing Catalogue

Which (if any) aspects of our advertising do you think are useful?
(Tick as many boxes as are relevant)

☐ Prices and publication dates of new editions

☐ Information on Text content

☐ Details of our free online offering

☐ None of the above

Your ratings, comments and suggestions would be appreciated on the following areas:

	Very useful	Useful	Not useful
Introductory section	☐	☐	☐
Quality of explanations	☐	☐	☐
How it works	☐	☐	☐
Chapter tasks	☐	☐	☐
Chapter Overviews	☐	☐	☐
Question Bank	☐	☐	☐
Index	☐	☐	☐

	Excellent	Good	Adequate	Poor
Overall opinion of this publication	☐	☐	☐	☐

Do you intend to continue using BPP Products?   ☐ Yes   ☐ No

Please note any further comments and suggestions/errors on the reverse of this page or e-mail them to: paulsutcliffe@bpp.com

Please return to: Paul Sutcliffe, Senior Publishing Manager, BPP Learning Media Ltd, FREEPOST, London, W12 8BR.

REVIEW FORM (continued)

TELL US WHAT YOU THINK

Please note any further comments and suggestions/errors below.